for few ... it was ... grand to have him with us ... talked for a good time to fix old car and have a ... that a new car in the future. As he was going home ... called on the phone and ... had a long conversation ... with later he called ... me ... a grand short ... talking with our grandchild... They allways wanted us to ...

Solo 5 MINUTI, ho detto...
cercherò di dirti che ...
non posso accusare la
colpa a teatro mia
messuno niente la
con un
bustetto in
piccolo
... con son
...

2 P.M.
I CAN
See
it is
SNOWING
And A
LITTLE
RAIN

Five
MINUTES
After 9
am
having
To Let
My Body
Relax
so I
can
Resume
My workout

NIGHT BLOOM

MARY CAPPELLO

A MEMOIR

BEACON PRESS

BOSTON

Beacon Press
25 Beacon Street
Boston, Massachusetts 02108-2892
www.beacon.org

Beacon Press books
are published under the auspices of
the Unitarian Universalist Association of Congregations.

03 02 01 00 99 98   8 7 6 5 4 3 2 1

This book is printed on recycled acid-free paper that contains at least 20
percent postconsumer waste and meets the uncoated paper ANSI/NISO
specifications for permanence as revised in 1992.

Text design by Elizabeth Elsas
Composition by Wilsted & Taylor Publishing Services

Library of Congress Cataloging-in-Publication Data

Cappello, Mary.
    Night bloom : a memoir / Mary Cappello.
        p.   cm.
    ISBN 0-8070-7216-8 (alk. paper)
        1. Cappello, Mary.   2. Italian Americans—Pennsylvania—Darby—
Biography.   3. Lesbians—Pennsylvania—Darby—Biography.
4. Darby (Pa.)—Biography.   I. Title.
CT275.C2794A3   1998
974.8'14—dc21   98-19582

TO MY BELOVED GUIDES,

Rosemary Petracca Cappello,

Jeannie Walton,

and Jack M. Payson

AND IN MEMORY OF

Ann Mauro (1968–1976),

little girl lost

. . . or an illness they had overcome when they were children begins again inside them; or a lost habit reappears, a certain hesitating turn of the head that was characteristic of them years before. And with what comes, a whole tangle of confused memories arises, hanging from it like wet seaweed on a sunken boat. Lives that you would never have known about bob to the surface and mingle with what really happened, and drive out a past that you thought you knew: for in what rises there is a new, rested strength, while what was always there is tired out from too much remembrance.

RAINER MARIA RILKE,
The Notebooks of Malte Laurids Brigge

CONTENTS

Slender Iris

I'm four years old in 1964. It's spring, and the air is indigo—indigo colored, indigo veiled, indigo scented. I can say this because my brothers, whom I envy for their daily journeys to school, have been teaching me what they've learned there: "Roy-G-Biv," my brother, Anthony, three years my elder, tells me, "is how you remember the colors of the rainbow: red, orange, yellow, green, blue, indigo, and violet." I picture Roy G. Biv as a Texan, or at least a cowboy: some gun-slinging, long-faced, lean, and tall-hatted figure bedizened with a rainbow-colored holster. I love his spurs. I'd like a pair myself. In my mind, I confuse the word "indigo"—my favorite rainbow color—with "Indian" or "Injun," and my brother laughingly corrects me when I each time inadvertently end the litany of colors that I, a preschooler, have mastered with the word "violent" rather than "violet." Underneath his rainbow camouflage, behind his gleaming Roy-to-the-rescue smile, Roy was violent. But, no, like every tried-and-true American child, I'd been learning that *Indians* were violent, the Indians, the indigo, who thanks to Roy were safely stowed in the vest pocket of his name.

Indigo was my favorite color because it seemed unallowed. It was an adult word, a sophisticated hue, not easily recognized in the real world of stiffly colored blocks, dipped then sealed at all corners in blue or saturated red. Indigo never appeared in the flash card question/answer series. If indigo reminded me of Indian, its referent was a particular Indian of whom I was fond—Tonto of the Lone Ranger television show. I loved Tonto's tanned and clean-shaven chest, and what kept me watching the show was the hope that once, just once, the Lone Ranger, who was suffocatingly overdressed—not only was his shirt buttoned up to his chin, but he had coverings on his head, eyes, and hands—would take off his clothes too and let Tonto swashbuckle him to the ground, naked male chest to naked male chest. (I watched the Superman series, as I suppose most people did, for related reasons, in the hope that Superman and Lois Lane would finally consummate.) There were no plains, no ranges or trails in the working-class town outside of Philadelphia where I was growing up, but my Lone Ranger-embraces-Tonto fantasies were aided by a prized possession that truly must have come from Santa Claus since my parents could never have afforded it: a black and white life-sized rocking horse named "Blaze." Blaze, the talking horse. You pulled a string at the base of his long sleek neck and he whinnied. You pulled again and he said, "I want some hay." Each morning, after I'd pretend-fed Blaze in the dark cellar of our Darby row home, I'd mount and rock him in accompaniment to the rhythms of my mother's washing, ironing, hanging, and folding clothes. I love this morning ritual, especially when I'm convinced that my play infects and lightens the doggedness of my mother's work. Unless my head is hurting from a nightmare that persists confusedly, painfully in the morning. As on this particular spring morning in my fourth year.

Instead of mounting Blaze, I try to climb into his lap and rest my head on his neck. I want him to wander, clippety-clop, clippety-clop, into a silent field, bending only to feed himself on dandelions, sniffing at a ray of light, patient with me, half sleeping in the color of my mood: indigo. I slide off the toy rocker listlessly this morning and tell my mother I'm going out to play. It's a spring day, but I decide I'd like to dress as though it's Halloween. Rummaging through the toy chest that is wedged between the hot water heater and the basement door that leads out of the house, I retrieve a dusty sheet. What once were eye and nose holes for a child ghost are rotted and ripped. I push my entire head through one hole and wear the sheet like a cape. I don a sword made of aluminum foil and cardboard that one of my brothers had made for his role in a grade-school version of *Julius Caesar*, and I complete the outfit with a papier-mâché mask resembling "Smokey the Bear," made, no doubt, by my oldest brother, Joe, for "Fire Prevention Week." I run out the back door, flailing the sword and growling. I jump in circles, "Grrr, grrr," swiping at the air, hoping to inspire fear in the other little kids I find in the driveway that separates our row of houses from our tiny backyards, but they can only double up with laughter at Smokey's stupid grin.

This is a day to play alone in. I don't want anyone, I decide, only the refuge of my father's garden. Half tripping, half climbing the five finely graded steps that are still too steep for me, I enter the garden. Everything seems shaded in indigo—the pansies, the crocuses, and especially my father's irises, his prize. Their stalks are slender and delicate but strong; they are luminous with grace, the direct result of my father's care. The edge of my costume sword is blunt, but it cuts through the stalks enough to dent and dampen them. These flowers will never blossom. After several whacks and "grrrs" directed at the air and at the iris, I flee, panting, to the back of the small brick fireplace my father has built at the far end of the yard. It seems I spend the whole afternoon there hiding behind my Smokey the Bear mask. Liking the way it envelopes my breath. Liking the way it smells of carnations. I have been having nightmares about my brother. In real life, my father beats him, sometimes with his hands, or with his belt, or with whatever objects happen to be at hand. My father beats both of my brothers this way, but he seems to have a special dislike for my oldest brother, his unoriginal namesake, Joe. His favorite humiliation is to kick my brother in his ass. I have scary dreams. In them, my father has shaved my brother's head. My brother sits in a corner with his shaved head, crying. His head is bloody; his head is bruised. Black and blue, black and blue, the color of indigo.

ONE

The Sweetness of Doing Nothing

Snapdragons, if you press the hairy underside of their throats ever so gently, will speak. As a child, I wanted to eat every blossom in my father's garden, until I learned the pleasure in my mouth of their names: calla lily, cosmos, rose eclipse, dahlia. As an adult, I keep *The Field Guide to Wild Flowers* on the same shelf with books of poems: "fragrant bedstraw," "wild madder," "grass-of-parnassus," "night-flowering catchfly," "ragged robin," "shooting star." My mother shared much of what grew in my father's garden with neighbors—even the ones who weren't speaking to her. It is 1968, and my mother's views on civil rights make her the local radical; her article appearing in the *Catholic Standard and Times* describing the paper as a "dismal rag" has not endeared her to our law-abiding Italian and Irish neighbors. Still my mother sends me at eight years old on the errand to deliver tomatoes in odd-sized brown paper bags to each unsuspecting asphalt dweller. Now there is something like the receipt of a letter to celebrate on Concord Road.

Turning down a particular garden path in my mind—it might be lined with shells or bricks, discarded tires or aluminum cans—I remember how gardens provide a way to wander, and how gardens become a place for the sweetness of doing nothing. After squeezing out orange juice for a family of nine, sizzling orange peel for scent, washing with arthritic fingers each sock on a washboard, my great-grandmother, Josephine Conte, disappears through the screen door of her son's house to the garden. She's left her rosaries behind, fills her pockets with camphor leaf, then sits or stands staring, not sighing now for her five dead children—Gesuel, Maddalena, Alfredo, Antonio, Edoardo—or for the ocean between her and the place of their birth and death. She walks slowly; she nods; she sits or stands. She's doing nothing. Turning another bend, beneath the pear tree whose fruit the squirrels have won again, stands Josephine's only remaining son, my grandfather, Giovanni Petracca, hands open, eyes shut. So many shoes repaired will mean at least one of his own children will be able to see the dentist. But for these moments, it is important to do nothing. In another generation, there's my mother. Locked in our row home for seven years with agoraphobia—episodes of which began in the Catholic Church she later learned to leave—my mother roams the garden at least, gathering herbs, gathering thoughts, she writes.

Neither the work of writing nor the intensity of gathering is what stands out to me in this memory, but, once again, perfect stillness and blessed inactivity. Watching my mother from our dining room window, or more likely, as a child in search of her, is it possible that I decide not to beckon her, but simply to enjoy this unusual vision of her at rest, at peace? Probably I did call to her, did interrupt her spell, because I knew this was a different space from her depression and that I wanted to share in that long, slow swim through pulsating color. I see my mother from all sides through the tunnel of memory's lens. My mother is still. My mother is clear. My mother is clearly quiescent. And even though the feeling is liquid, my mother does not dissolve in this memory of the garden so much as she resolves, is resolved, finds momentary resolution in the shade of a cherry tree or as she bends to break a sprig of parsley or, buoyed up by a trail of roses by her side, looks up to the sky. On the other hand, lately I have dreams. I dream the grain of my father's garden as though I'm screening a home movie of the garden in the dream. In this dream, the garden is lush, but I can only tell this by its patches of color, not by scent or touch or weather. This seems significant. My father poses before the garden's entrance, before the slopes of prickly pear cemented by my great-uncle Tony. The garden, though a blur, is clear, but my father seems ghostly, and I don't know how to make him materialize. I know and love my father's garden but I don't know him, and our love for each other was stemmed even before it could bud, let alone blossom.

The earth the gardener digs in and the root systems he tends are attached in complex ways to a house or an idea of a house, to a neighborhood, to a state flower, to the landscape of the country that he has left if he is an immigrant, to the gardens of familial patriarchs and matriarchs. In my family, three such gardens glimmered in place of family jewels: my father's, my maternal grandfather's, and that of my great-uncle by marriage, Antonio Polidori. A great-grandfather's garden that predated these was supposed to have yielded the most spectacular scenes of all. But the ancestors who survived to greet my generation surrounded the memory of my maternal great-grandfather with a deafening silence. Were they really "doing nothing" in the glorious silence that their gardens allowed? Or were they conjuring him so as to bury him? That gardener's flowers I never glimpsed, though sometimes as a child I swore I saw a man with blooms pressed to his heart, his mouth, his eyes, dancing a floral dance, struggling to make himself come clear and glorious in my grandfather's backyard.

———

June 20, 1943. Father's Day! Saw the new day at exactly 6:30. The sky is clear and much promising. Cut my back yard hedge planted many years ago by my father who is in heaven now. Pruned a tree.

FROM THE JOURNAL OF JOHN PETRACCA

My maternal great-grandfather, Antonio Petracca, father of John Petracca, was a master gardener. The first of my family to emigrate from Teano in southern Italy before calling his wife and sixteen-year-old son to join him—the year was 1916— Antonio made a modest living in the United States by keeping the wealthy warm: in the summertime, he landscaped the gardens of the families who lived on Philadelphia's Main Line; in the winter, he took care of their furnaces. Every year, Ardmore, the town where he lived, sponsored a gardening contest, and every year, I'm told, my great-grandfather's garden took the prize. I don't know what distinguished my great-grandfather's garden. No one seems ever to have photographed it, and in all the reams of jottings that his son left behind, no description of his father's garden abides. What I know about the man himself is shrouded in mystery, a source of family shame or family pity. However judged, his was certainly the greatest of family secrets.

Straining my ears to catch the meaning of my family's whispers, I heard of two misdeeds attached to his character. Some said that he was a gigolo—the exact word used to describe him—an irresistibly attractive dancer (and in this sense, according to Webster, a literal gigolo) who was unfaithful to my great-grandmother when she was pregnant with my grandfather. They said that he, along with wife and child, was exiled from my grandfather's birthplace because of a death and possible murder that bore some connection to an illicit love affair. Whether the woman involved invited his advances or whether he forced himself upon her was never clear. Great-grandmother Josephine Conte had ways of dealing with what could not be spoken. She would, for example, open the neckline of her dress and talk down into it, as if she were telling her troubles to her own heart. And when that didn't work, my mother told me, she would go to a place she'd never been before and leave her troubles there. She did, however, share shards of her experience, the base of her own trauma, with her daughter-in-law, Rose Arcaro, as they together cared for Rose's children. Rose, in turn, presumably sworn to secrecy, occasionally unburdened herself of the tale, morsel by morsel, but she never gave the whole to any one person.

That the story reeks of the worst stereotyping of Italian character—a Gothic narrative with passion and murder at its center—keeps whatever might be real and useful in it at bay. Nor is my knowledge of this enigmatic point of departure helped by the fact that on those rarest of rare occasions, in those weak moments when my grandmother was compelled to tell of what she knew of it, she'd keep me from hearing by talking to my mother in Italian. But even my mother was kept from the real, the full, the true story. All that my mother could tell me for sure was that my grandfather was forever estranged from his father, who after all had abandoned him and his mother in more ways than one. In addition to failing to be loyal to my great-grandmother, who had also suffered the loss of all her children but one, my great-grandfather failed to make clear when he left for the United States that he would eventually send for Josephine and John. When he felt surer of his footing in the United States, he sent her a telegram requesting that she send to him his son. My great-grandmother made the journey even though she was not called for. My grandfather, by this time nearing sixteen years old, became in a sense his mother's protector; he sympathized with her suffering and tried to give her a better life in the home he was making with his wife, Rose, after his father died. I'd also heard that my great-grandfather's illegitimate child was killed in an accident and that the townspeople blamed my great-grandfather for the child's death.

My mother presented a different version of the story, or a different piece, on each occasion that I asked her for more details. It was hard to discern whose need the story most spoke to now, for the teller each piece originated with was hopelessly lost in the intermingled strands offered mainly by the women in my family: great-grandmother tells my grandmother who tells my mother who compares what she knows with her sisters. Running alongside this confused pattern is the border of my grandfather's grave silence and his dinnertime rituals. Dinner at the Petraccas was an occasion marked by humility and thankfulness; it had the bearing of a minimalist aesthetic colored by the care put into the meal. Picture for dessert a pear, crudely sculpted, delicately peeled by my grandfather's penknife. If in place of a pear, a peach, the ritual would lose its delicacy and be shadowed by a cloud of bravado, for my grandfather had the uncanny habit of cutting to the center of a peach, and, depending on the temperature or temperament of the day, opening the peach's inner cabinet as though it were a locket or shucking it as though it were a clam. Then he would extract the smaller seed that was nestled like a bead of knowledge inside the outer stone and swallow it as one might an after-dinner medicinal. Certain folk remedies prescribe a little poison for a great pain, but when I learned that peach seeds bore traces of arsenic, I couldn't help but wonder if my grandfather was killing himself in minute degrees or at least testing his fortitude in a way that made eating dessert into a game of truth or dare. Would he ever tell the truth about his father? Could he ever know?

The most recent version of the story that I receive from my mother is not overshadowed by a possible accident, a possible murder, but marked by a very definite encounter. A woman in the village beckons my great-grandmother to her house, she doesn't know what for. When she arrives, the woman takes my great-grandmother to the edge of a tiny coffin. Therein lies a baby, the woman's child and the child of my great-grandmother's husband, the woman explains. There is no murder; there is no accident. What's important here is this meeting between two women over another of my great-grandfather's dead children. The mistress wants to use the death to convey to my great-grandmother her pain; to convey what a louse her husband is; to convey the curse they share in loving him or in letting him love them, or in letting him have them. My great-grandmother is pregnant with my grandfather at this time, and even though they both survive, I picture my great-grandmother laying herself down then and there to die. But this is only because, continually in doubt of my own fortitude, I am perpetually amazed by other people's ability to live through pain. Ever in search of strategies, I beg friends and strangers to tell me in as much detail and with as much precision as possible how they cope. I like to think of my grandfather's survival of infancy and childhood as a testament to my great-grandmother's decision to cease to live in and through her husband and his passions, the beginning of my grandfather's life as an act of her will. What she could not foresee was how through this son's children, she might in part be healed. In a journal entry dated April 12, 1942, my grandfather writes:

Today is my mother's birthday. I am so happy that the day is beautiful and that everyone is doing his best to make mother happy. When I came back from work I saw Frances and little Rosemary fixing a basket full of azaleas. They motioned to me not to let anyone in the house know it. Later they marched in both holding the basket singing Happy Birthday to Grandma. It was simply grand. Mother kissed them both. I believe, besides mother's blowing the candles out on the cake ahead of time, their act was the best.

In what sense did she blow the candles out ahead of time? Maybe she didn't want "Happy Birthday" sung to her twice; maybe she didn't want more attention drawn to her, since for every person consoled, there is someone else in search of consolation—the mistress this story leaves behind, for example. Did great-grandmother and this woman love each other before that terrible encounter and the circumstances that led up to it, and did this meeting kill their love? Or did they begin to love each other then? Or are these questions that only a lesbian great-granddaughter would ask? For every person consoled, there is someone else in search of consolation. Great-grandfather died young. No one would ever say of what, but in the preparation of this writing, my mother tells me that he died, of course, of that unspeakable scourge, of syphilis. I realize that not only is Great-grandfather marked as the source of the family's immutable sadness, but that his character fuels an unspoken fear: that syphilis killed each of his children as well, except my grandfather, who kept a peach tree so that he might always have its medicine at hand.

An unutterable deed haunts one side of my great-grandfather's portrait, on the other side, a bright spot, his garden. What I know about my great-grandfather is a bright spot and a burdensome enigma underwritten by violence and pain, the pain he may have caused others. And that my family inherited his hedge.

In the mid-1950s, my mother, though she had won medals for her achievements in high school Latin and was already gaining recognition from her teachers for her writing abilities, graduated from her high school's commercial course. Like her four sisters, excepting the eldest two, who had entered the convent together, she was expected to find employment in the business world as soon as possible after high school, or to marry. By the time my mother met my father, she had managed to save some money from her job as a secretary at radio station WHAT in Philadelphia. Though she'd considered using her small savings to visit Italy, her decision to marry led her to use this money for the down payment on a dirt cheap row home in need of repairs in Darby, Pennsylvania, about twenty miles from the town where she grew up. The row homes were standard dwellings for a working-class suburb: twenty two-story units were directly joined one to the other, with a front walkway shared by each pair of houses. Each house was lucky to come with a small patch of grass in front of it and a somewhat larger backyard, separated from the house by a tarred back lane. In many cases, neighbors opted to cement over one or the other if not both of the grassy extensions to their houses.

The backyard of the house that my parents moved into was overrun with weeds, except where a path had been worn by people who had used the yard as a shortcut. As my mother tells it, one particularly gargantuan weed took up the entire width of the yard, and a cluster of wild cherry trees made the space unsuitable for a garden in need of light. My mother knew she wanted a garden here, but it was men not women who took charge of the garden in my family's Italian American households, and my father, who grew up in the Sicilian section of South Philadelphia in an even tinier row home, sans garden, did not know the first thing about tending one. Though my mother played a central role in the realization of the garden and in its continuance, the garden's care and upkeep became in many ways my father's preserve. He learned by watching my mother's father and my Uncle Tony, husband to Ann, my maternal grandmother's sister, and by reading. The results he achieved in his garden shocked his family who now failed to recognize him when they'd visit: who would have expected to find Joe, their brother who hadn't finished high school, now reading seed catalogs; who would have thought that Joe, with all of his impatiences, would come to enjoy starting seedlings painstakingly under special lights in his garage?

My mother employed Uncle Tony to get their garden started. He made a fence for the garden, removed most of the cherry trees, evened out the terrain, and, following his trade, cemented a pristine set of steps leading into the garden graced with a cemented slope on either side. He finished the job with a gift by planting the first plants for my parents in the slopes that formed the new entrance to the yard: myrtle, alyssum, evergreen, and ground cover pinks.

Now it was time for the front yard to gain its special border, and my grandfather came with wishes for good health as he planted cuttings from his father's hardy hedge around the three edges of the small front yard. The hedge that my great-grandfather had originally transplanted to my grandfather's garden from his own held a verbal if not literal place of honor there. To this day, I cannot picture the part of my grandfather's garden where his father's hedge grew: so *open* is the picture of my grandfather's garden in my mind's eye, so *wildly* well kept and dazzling is the imprint of his garden's scene, that I fail to see a hedge there at all. I only remember the reverence with which the hedge was spoken of by my mother and grandfather, and how it was the one feature of the garden whose origin must be remarked: "Great-grandfather's hedge," or "the hedge that was originally planted by Great-grandfather." It was as though this dignified shrub enabled its owners to concur that Antonio Petracca wasn't entirely a louse: he *had* given them something; he had saved something special for them from the bounty of his wiles, something that could help them in the new world in which they struggled to survive.

Not generally acknowledged like flowering bushes or plants for their warmth or beauty, hedges mark enclosures and draw distinctions. The hedge might have been the metaphoric border that was supposed to keep my family's gardens from intermingling—each in its way hoeing its own row toward an idea of class mobility. If the hedge was a tool for marking differences, it was one my grandfather was more beset by than willing to apply, for his own identity had been shaped too harshly by divisions that included citizen/alien, English-speaker/Italian-speaker, middle class/poor. Still my grandfather spoke with veneration of his father's hedge.

My mother, as guardian of its second incarnation before her house, took to her hedge with a ferocity that, while it never exactly smacked of violence, certainly seemed electrified by a force within my mother that she couldn't otherwise express. As keeper of the hedge, my mother's job was to periodically trim it, which she did in those days with long-edged wood-handled shears as opposed to electric blades. The job took muscle, and my mother trimmed the entire hedge at once without pause. Those shears snapped out the rhythm of the heady rhapsody that was her sweaty, therapeutic workout, though not, as one might surmise, on a designated schedule of Mondays or first Fridays. Nor did the ritual wait on weather, but followed by necessity the ebb and flow, or more accurately, the fever pitch of frustration reached in conversations with her husband or her mother or her parish priest (my mother was still in those years in search of emotional, intellectual, and social sustenance from the Catholic Church). When she called her mother in desperation over what she was learning about the man she'd married—especially about his unpredictable temper and his unwillingness to change—when she told her mother that she wanted to leave, her mother would reply: "You made your bed, now sleep in it." When she sought guidance from the mother superior or priest at Blessed Virgin Mary Church, they listened obligingly to her accounts of loneliness and nervousness, then reminded her that in light of the Greater crucifixion, "Your problem, Mrs. Cappello, is that you are a sinner." Following such suffocations, my mother trimmed her hedge as though to breathe. Smothered, she did not shout, but rapped out a refrain several hours' long: "Fuck this fucking hedge" and the shameful story it will never yield; "Fuck this fucking hedge" and the paternal body it pretends to shield; "Fuck this fucking hedge," symbol of containment, of what keeps me in, of what I cannot leave or leave behind.

My generation's relation to this nondescript plant, great-grandfather's hedge, had its own remarkable qualities. Quite literally, the hedge was something that cushioned us; more abstractly, it proved a soundproof grate that braced our confessions. On a number of occasions, when my friends and I would play too roughly, the hedge would break our fall. Its branches didn't stick or prick their assailant; they would give like the easy snapping of twigs even though the plant was succulent, and its tiny waxen leaves would cling to the backs of our legs like so many Band-Aids or bingo chips. In our teenage years, my friends and I would sit on the three front steps by the hedge to discuss the seriousness of our confusions, our desire for different pleasures, or the helplessness we felt about the conflicts in our households. My good friend Cathy, admitting to herself for the first time and to me that both of her parents were alcoholic but were not willing to admit it to themselves or to her, plucked leaves from the hedge between sentences, stared into the center of their nearly heart-shaped edges to find a word, then tore them slowly into confetti that fell to the ground with her tears. My mother, angered to find leafless gaps in the hedge after my talks with Cathy, would command me to sweep the steps.

If I really want to remember how the hedge functioned for me though, I must enter afternoons marked by inexplicable revelations—revelations that were enabled by my older brother, Anthony. I must be willing to remember my brother.

To my child's eye, the hedge is haunted. It is a net, an intricacy, a Bermuda Triangle into which things—toys or limbs—might disappear. On so many occasions I have lost things; on so many occasions those things have shown up in the hedge. Or, rather, my brother finds them there, this litany of missing parts whose loss has made me treat the games they belong to as defunct: a single white shoe from my nurse doll (I can't fancy her treading her imaginary hospital halls barefoot); the hollow pink rubber ball we hit against the three front steps in a game called "step ball"; Monopoly bills blown from the short table on the adjacent patch of patio; shuttlecocks; the most important, the black, pick-up stick; the key to my skates. On any number of interminable afternoons of nothing but regret—none of my games are playable—my brother spots a missing piece in the hedge. We're staring at the same hedge, or so I think, when he makes out among its brambles the shape of a sphere, or line, or pendant rectangle, hook, or cone. He is the one who finds toys in the hedge, just as he is the one, in the wooded walks we take along the nearby creek, to spot deer tracks, find birds' nests, or a chameleonic mushroom, or, each year as autumn approaches, to discover in the hedge the well-camouflaged presence of a praying mantis. My brother never acts as excited as I think he should when he makes these discoveries—it is just how he sees the world—whereas his findings always profoundly alter the quality of my day. They fill me with excitement, and you can hear me ringing "Thank you, thank you, thank you" in his ears.

I practiced reading the hedge through the children's magazine *Highlights* "Seek 'n' Find" puzzles, which asked you to find the boot hidden in the image of a tree, or the rabbit's ear among the shrubbery, or the button doubling as a knot in the wooded floorboard. But somehow this didn't translate directly outdoors into sighting missing pleasures in the master shrub. Whenever my brother pointed the found object out to me, I would feel bathed in "but-of-courseness." It was like shifting your optic to see the lady *and* the goblet, the duck *and* the rabbit in those two-toned visual conundrums. Once I saw what my brother saw, I realized none of my playthings was really ever *hidden* in the hedge. I just wasn't where I had to be to see them.

I loved what my brothers taught me, and for the most part, in spite of inevitable rivalries, I loved having brothers. Though neither of my brothers was very macho—if Anthony was ridiculed for his slight physique, Joe was for his gentle doughboy body—I always, happily, could dissuade my own attackers with the line: "You'd better stop, or I'll get my brother after you." Joe taught me how to visualize multiplication tables by holding up before my eyes the palms of his open hands as he chanted five times five times five. He taught me how to tie my shoes, and how to ride a bike. Anthony taught me how to roll my "r's" and how to drop first one then a stack of pennies from my elbow and catch it in the same hand. Both of my brothers were "smart," and each school year I dreaded the inevitable recognition that would come immediately after the teacher had pronounced my last name—"You must be Joe and Anthony's sister": expectations for brilliance were thereby set.

By the time I was in high school, Anthony, who was known in our neighborhood by the name of "yolk," short for "egghead," was thought of as the family genius. In those years, he taught me calculus so well that I botched the teacher's lesson plans. Mr. Goodwin would assign us problems that we were meant to spend a week on in the class. I'd bring the problem to my brother who didn't solve it for me so much as he talked me through it. Calculus, I discovered, bore a relation to geometry. To solve most problems, I had to discern previously unrecognized shapes—another version of finding things in the hedge. Calculus got me to think of the world in terms of shapes in space, space and its limits, proofs of the existence of such shapes and their interdependence. My calculus teacher and the rest of the class would be stunned when I laid out the solution to each problem across the length of several boards and then explained it. Mr. Goodwin would then wax poetic about the beauty of calculus and how my solution wasn't bad for a girl, "and at that an Italian," he'd add, then make some joke about my spaghetti sauce and whether that was just as good. I never took offense at Mr. Goodwin's comments because I knew he was genuinely pleased with the seriousness with which I took his subject—and because I felt he was secretly jealous of my ability to explain more clearly than he could the solution of a problem. The more I learned in the areas of math and science, the more convinced I became that these subjects were not unusually hard. They were just rarely accompanied by someone who could communicate their ways and means. I taught my peers in high school and then, in light of my brother's guidance, tutored calculus in college.

In the meantime, though, I somehow lost track of my brother. He'd dropped out of the electrical engineering program he was enrolled in at Drexel University near our home in Philadelphia; I had made the break to live on campus at Dickinson College in Carlisle, where I intended to double major in English and chemistry and write the first coherent chemistry textbook. Our maternal grandfather, though immensely learned because self-taught, left Italy with the formal equivalent of a fourth-grade education; our father had not finished high school. We were the first to venture into higher education. Anthony kept his co-op job in the lab of a local brewery for a short time, but then started to withdraw. In the ensuing years, my parents divorced, and he withdrew even more. For a long time, he couldn't hold a job or leave the house much. Though he finally got therapy and kept a full-time job as a stockperson at an auto parts supply store, some form of what seems like woundedness has persisted: he has profound difficulty communicating with other people, and lives with my father still in the house we grew up in. He restricts his social life to seeing my mother on weekends and playing with his brother's daughter and son. Anthony, who had the longest memory in the family—he would remember colors and clothes and who said what, and when and where, from events that for the rest of us were hopelessly blurred—now seems unable to imagine a future.

I don't know how my brother who was the family angel—all benignity and humor, the only person who could make my mother laugh—got lost. Did he get lost, or is it just that I am no longer able to find him? When I looked for him, he was no longer in the place he used to be: older, wiser brother, teacher with a second sight, with a knack for finding things. Now he was silent and unreachable. How was it that the brother who had walked me by talking me through calculus problems now seemed congenitally unable to talk? How could he have become such a different person than the boy I knew? What had happened or had been happening? Maybe instead of helping me with my high school math, he should have been doing his own university assignments. Ever making discoveries for someone else.

Was my brother developmentally disabled and we all failed to see it? Was my brother immobilized by some aspect of my family's dysfunction in a way none of us could afford to see or know? Should my mother have been worried rather than delighted when my brother as a child showed a tendency toward writing upside down and backwards? I remain forever thankful to my brother for how he transmuted fragments—one part gravity, one part accident, one part neglect—into a shape I could discern in Great-grandfather's hedge. Great-grandfather was my mother's family's secret. My brother Anthony is mine.

CHAPTER 2

The Translations of John Petracca

*I must look at life upside down if I want to see my ideas
come true.*

*There was a man, shabby in every detail, aged but very alert,
standing before a four way crossing, thinking aloud.*

FROM THE JOURNAL OF JOHN PETRACCA

Perhaps because his mother was a weaver, my grandfather's
garden took the shape of different bands of light placed side by
side. A series of strips laid down and juxtaposed, this garden
was a paean to alongsideness. It spoke to the difficulty of and
desire for coexistence; it extended metaphorically the short
threshold between work and home—my grandfather's shoe repair shop was attached to his house. The wide store window

faced a fairly busy Llanarch street and provided great pools of light for the plants my grandfather lined his window with. A clever, yellowed ad hung there as well: "You will wear out your shoes looking for a better place to repair them. Guaranteed work at a fair price." A person entering the store would usually find my grandfather repairing shoes, but they might also glimpse him in the act of writing—mountains of lore, short stories, aphorisms that he composed and jotted onto the material of his trade, whole treatises squeezed onto the back of the tab used to mark down what part of the shoe needed fixing, with a word inevitably broken by the hole-punched "O" at the top or bottom of the tab:

THE COBBLER'S DREAM

It was an April day, if I recall perfectly it was the first day of the month. What a day . . . April the fool! But the day was pretty. The sun was shining and the birds were singing not excluding seeing the flowers peeping out of their buds when I entered the dilapidated old shoe repair shop of my cobbler that for years he had served me satisfactorily.

He was curved over his bench attentively reading the morning paper.

"Good morning Dan," I greeted him.

"Good morning Mrs. Cook," he answered kindly.

"Are my shoes ready?"

"Not yet. I am sorry."

"But why don't you work?"

"Well I have become somewhat very slow because business is very poor and I have only your shoes to repair and I love to see a pair of shoes in the store."

"But what are you reading? News, sports, or funnies?"

"I am not reading the paper. See here is a little sheet typed by a young boy who dreams to be a writer and he makes a lot of sense. I always encourage him and he is so glad and thanks me . . . "

My grandfather did not leave his writing "in order," and so it is hard to know what he meant for it. Having arrived in the United States in 1916, already by 1925, at the age of twenty-five, he had written and published a novella in serial form entitled *Il Segreto di un Destino* (The Secret of a Destiny) in a local Italian (American) newspaper, *La Gazzetta Calabrese* (The Calabrian Gazette). I only know this because a portion of the crumbling newspaper in which the first installment of the book appeared lay among my grandfather's life's writings. I cannot read the story because I never learned the language—instead, bona fide product of assimilation, I have a Ph.D. in English. My grandfather also published a novel in Italian, but only my mother remembers the fact of its existence. She doesn't know what it was called, what subject it treated, who published it, or how young my grandfather was when he wrote it, but she remembers how it fit neatly into one of the numerous cubbyholes of the wonderfully large and intricate desk that he kept in a part of his shoe repair shop—the shop attached to the house they lived in. A door at the back of the store opened into the living room, which followed in a straight line to the dining room and kitchen. A jog to the left took one into a small screened-in back porch and then to the garden, where, right outside the kitchen window, the furthest point from the window that opened into the store, a fig tree thrived. A slender gravel driveway abutted the house to the left, but even this was lush. In fact, the garden's emphasis on inlaid strips—a patch of grass for social gatherings, a rectangle of earth for blooms and vegetables, a row of trees—made the driveway seem habitable in its own way, so much more than a slot to hold a car. The driveway, companionate and yet distinct, teemed with its own life. In a journal entry that my grandfather composed in the shadow of the Depression era and the trauma of impoverishment from which he never fully recovered, he describes a pretend birthday, set in the driveway, flecked with light:

Life is simply childish with me at this time. Just imagine, my little girl Frances sitting in the side yard of my home near me, under the lovely sun rays which, at the present time, 2 PM Sunday of 29, 1936, are shining majestically, asked me to light a match so she may blow it out. This is fun. I light matches and she blows them out.

The Italian novel vanished. According to my mother, after my grandfather died in the early 1970s, a cousin of mine who had both a literary bent and a leaning toward sundry forms of monkhood, asked for the book, but he claims no memory of the bequest now. (Perhaps it disappeared in one of his many vows to cast off worldly possessions.) The need and desire of my grandfather to learn English had altered the course of his literary output. He tried writing fiction in English now, and at some point in his younger days attended classes in fiction writing at the Franklin Annex in Philadelphia. My grandfather hoped to be a writer, and he was. My grandfather hoped to express his thoughts and feelings in the language of the new culture he had entered, but this presented a variety of problems. "'In vain!'" he writes, "Many are the pages that I have soiled but many too are hours that I have toiled in trying to convey my thoughts in a medium strange to me." To be a laborer and a writer in this culture was not allowed; there were no means by which his writing could become public. He wore the mantle of English uncomfortably; sometimes English simply was not adequate to his task.

Over the years, my grandfather continued to tinker with stories that he wrote in English, many of which he went to the trouble to make typescripts of, which he then drafted and redrafted, began again and left off again. He was between languages for the rest of his life, and the form that he turned to with the most vigor and consistency was not fiction, but an ever-changing system of journal keeping and making. In some periods, his journal is kept in small notebooks where the chronology is easy to make out. But for the most part his jottings—urbane, poetic, reverential as daily prayers, philosophical—are scored onto whatever errant piece of paper happens to be at hand when the desire to write comes. Though the desire is often a daily one, and the thoughts express a certain urgency, there does not seem much of an attempt to place the writing in a self-contained space or even to acknowledge that the compositions might bear some relation to each other. Some pieces —mounds of odd-sized paper bits with writing on them—he collected into shoe boxes marked on the outside with the words: "Fragments of erratic thoughts from Llans Cobbler."

As far as I know, my grandfather never read these pieces to or attempted to share them with anyone, though he did know fellow artists in both the mandolin and guitar orchestra and the social club that he helped to found. My mother knew all her life of my grandfather's writing, and even when she was a child she read what he wrote without his knowing it. Or maybe he did know it, and she, the youngest and only of his six children to show interest in books, was his projected audience. More likely, this was his letter to the world that never wrote to him.

It would be interesting to trace when and to know why my grandfather moved from one language to another. When he writes about the war, my mother, who can read a little Italian, tells me, he shifts to Italian. But there is enough that is mysterious about my grandfather's writing in the language that I do understand to keep me in an eternal state of wonder. Visually, the journals appear as improvised clock faces. Rather than record each new entry to conform to a predetermined left to right, top to bottom line, John Petracca shifted the line each day by turning the page to a different angle before he began to write. Each entry appears like a smaller or larger number on the clock face of the page, and I am compelled, therefore, to read the passages in clockwise manner, turning the page, like a sequin of time, as I go. This leads me to picture my grandfather as a collagist, whose page turned toward him at a different angle each day, and who kept recording because of a faith that the right angle would be found out in time.

Each time I am presented with the visual enigma—the visual splendor—of such pages, I intuit a different image to clarify their form. One day it is clear they are timepieces; other days they're clearly imagined gardens with each square of words a seedbed; sometimes the collages seem all about seams, quiltlike; other times they are sculpted and inlaid weights and balances, a webwork of interdependencies that defy the law of gravity—I can't see what's holding them together, but I know it's there. Gazing at one page, for example, in the attitude of an abstractionist, I can't help noticing two miniature "pieces" of writing that have been wedged into some of the free space between the passages that serve as points on a clock face. I assume that the words etched onto these tiny rhymed columns must be significant because they seem to have been placed just so, consoling lights balanced on the edge of time's spinning wheel. Taking my keenest vision to them—the words are tiny—I read: "Five minutes of rest I am having to let my body relax so I can resume my work," and "2 PM I can see hailing, snowing and little rain." At first I think, "So much for that; these words are nothing of note," but in the next instant, a voice tells me to look again, and I am tuned to the surprise of what they record. They are the punctuations, the pauses, the breaths in my grandfather's work day. They are a form of sacred time, tiny, and full of life. Immediately, for reasons I can't entirely explain, I have a different kind of revelation with regard to the journals' form. I understand them now as having the shape of poverty. Each entry is written at a different angle so that it will take up less room, so that my grandfather may conserve paper. At various times he remarks it, a condition beyond my ken—

how he cannot afford to buy a writing tablet. Whether the words actually take up less space in their collage configuration than they would if he followed a standard linear format is neither here nor there; what is important is that the angle of his entries gives the illusion of space, it makes the page seem bigger than it is. My grandfather's page is like an overcrowded tenement. This tells me, especially in light of my fancy theorizing, that I lack the resources, I do not have the means to value my grandfather's writing for what it is.

Sometime in the late sixties, my grandparents, due to financial strain, cease to own a car. My father parks in the driveway when we visit now, and each leave-taking is surrounded by a driveway ritual. My grandparents' good-byes don't stop at the door to the house. No matter what the weather, they come out and stand before the car as my father slowly backs it out. They walk in slow synchrony toward us; they perform this slow dance that they've mastered down the length of the driveway. Sometimes they wave and smile; other times they simply walk and watch; sometimes their arms are linked, sometimes they're folded, other times they're resting by their sides. The ritual makes my father uncomfortable—he's convinced us it's dangerous to stand in front of or follow on foot a moving car, and he seems to be afraid of accidentally moving forward rather than backward during some good-bye and mowing them down. I always wave at my grandparents no matter their posture or the mood of the visit. Then I watch from the back window for as long as I can see them but never long enough to see them return to the house. Growing along the side of the driveway are forget-me-nots. My mother names them for me once as we prepare to leave, and I say, "*They're* forget-me-nots?" I remember being disappointed and surprised to learn that those particular flowers, quiet and small, were the real life match for that magical name: "forget-me-nots." I'd expected a grand flower, one that would scream from the plant: "Remember me!" But these flowers said remembering required effort and attention, because the pinpricks of our existence were so tiny and precious they could easily be erased by a passing wind.

January 2, 1945. It is cold, cold and cold. Our home, due to the many cracks that time has cruelly created, cannot get warm. My mother feels cold, my wife feels cold, and I too am feeling cold. Furthermore, to make things worse, Rosemary and Frances, sent home from school that the local could not become warm, they too protest cold. What am I to do? Cry? Indeed not. But, although I feel bitter towards the whole thing, I am laughing and dancing all over the rooms. Trying to keep warm and inspire gaiety so the rest could snap out of their grimace and become happy and warm in spite of all the adversities that poverty drags along mercilessly.

February 6, 1942. May God forgive this avaricious humanity that worships cold!

FROM THE JOURNAL OF JOHN PETRACCA

Let us gather to ourselves / In harvest / The heady autumn air / The fluted dahlias / The white blooms of basil / The final figs / Let us save them from / Frost

FROM ''FROST WILL COME''
BY ROSEMARY PETRACCA CAPPELLO

My great-grandfather made a living keeping wealthy people's furnaces aflame and tending their gardens. In the aftermath of the Depression, his son's house will never be warm. Warmth persists for me as an aesthetic goal—the desire to conjure warmth from words—even when what is important to me on other levels and in other places changes. I must produce warmth with my words if I am to coax my ancestors out of their shadows, because what is most apparent about the trouble they are in is that it chills them. My grandfather's house is frequently cold. There may be only a handful of words in the English language to refer to temperatures that are below those required to maintain human life, but "cold" in my grandfather's journals assumes countless forms: from the fact of the cold that invades his body to cold as the abstract monster he tries to tame with metaphor; from the "colds" that cold brings to the coldness he fears becoming; from cold's tendency to shrink the space one inhabits to cold's ability to open space, to demolish doors, making the room seem too big, and one's body too terribly small for the room's bare and freezing expanse. Given cold's multiple, mutable forms, warmth is hardly a simple antidote.

Cold comes once a year, but lasts anywhere from three to six months in the northeastern part of the United States.

October 10, 1941. Finally rain has arrived. The draught has been broken, but cold now is on our neck. Rigid weather is another pest to us poors! We have no umbrellas, no raincoats, and no good roof! Our shelter facing bad weather is in a very deplorable condition. Do I shiver in realizing all this? Only God knows.

October 11, 1941. It is cold. My ears burn. The store here is too chilly but I must stand it. I have been offered a job on a breadwagon. I guess I'll take it. 24 long years here is more than enough. I must try life anew. This reminds me of Dante: "Per navigar miglior acque alzi le veli, ormai la navicella del mio ingenio, che lascia indietro a se sì mar crudele!" *[To sail on better waters the little ship of my intellect now raises its sails, leaving behind it such a cruel sea!]*

January 13, 1960. Rain, sleet, snow, cold, damp and what not—Headaches, pains, empty pockets, the roof leaks, need coal, mate needs eye glasses and I need everything. Life is for the rich, sorry to say, but it is the truth! The poor only exist; although they bear everything, they get very little.

September 28, 1961. Winter is not far off. I shiver waiting, for winter is so healthy and pretty but it changes if you are poor.

Through one small window of my grandfather's journal, I see my mother sick with a cold as a child:

March 1, 1942. Made a table lamp for my children from an old floor one. It answers the purpose well. My little Rosemary has a very bad cold. She has barked like a little pup all night long. It is a pity. Especially when I feel the room so cold! But God is with us.

To have a cold in a cold room is sad and scary, but my grandfather begins to treat the condition with more than his faith—with humor and poetry:

January 8, 1960. Cold and clear is the beginning of this day. My beloved has a good whopper of a cold. I myself am not too hot. But the coldest section of my domain is my pocket. What a wonderful feeling! Chained am I from the tip of my nose to the nails of my toes.

With a distinct generosity of heart, my grandfather tries to make meaning out of the senselessness that cold beats into him, but occasionally his metaphors edge up to the extremity of cold's perverseness. Coldness makes the rooms his family inhabits feel uncanny.

February 26, 1942. Weather mild. I have been tapping for nine long hours with a heavy cold. I cannot tell how I resisted. It must be my supreme will to provide for my family! My Anthony has a cold, too. My wife has a terrific headache. I have a cat that loves music. He walks to and fro on our piano keyboard any time that he has a chance to.

The cold has gotten under his skin:

June 19, 1944. Very stormy weather and hot. At one time it was so dark that it resembled twilight. I need shoes, my children need shoes, and what not, but when I realize that the end of the month is coming closer, I feign ignorance. I don't know what a monster I must appear to my innocent ones when they ask and I remain cold, even if my inside boils. Some day they will know, but I hope like a dream!

December 14, 1961. Terrific cold but very much clear. I froze waiting for the trolley. It is now 9:30 and my legs still feel cold. It is my fault because instead of dress for the winter I am still using the same clothes as I use for summer. Funny is it not? Is it negligence or is it depression?

May 17, 1961. Cooler but clear. The day is grand. The work here at the bank is fair, but my brain hammers without mercy. To lead a good life is a terrific struggle. I feel hot but I wish I felt cold! To be cold is to be in peace.

October 30, 1961. Very good weather but I feel worst than ever did! Will I survive? Who knows? Yet I am working and shall keep on till . . . ? Ho, please my good Lord spare me till my mission is complete and then put me to sleep like my good and sweet mother used to do when I was a child.

In these passages, my grandfather tries to picture death as desirable precisely because these many years the cold has inspired fear, a fear of death. It is not, therefore, surprising that a good deal of the record of his days is punctuated by his own or his loved ones' quickening pulse: nervousness, fainting, pounding heart, the body gone haywire, a rudderless ship, mood swings, wreckage, fears of the damage to his children's eyes as they study their lessons around a meagerly lit table, are coupled with his desire for steadiness, sweetness, and peace. In search of an attitude to strike toward his nervousness, my grandfather continually applies forgiveness. Forgiveness is one of my grandfather's keynotes. It's the dose of goodness he will grant himself in an attempt to feel human in a world that denies him full humanity. He reminds himself of this ethic by encoding it in many of the stories he records—especially in those accounts of people who deny members of his community employment. Such people are to be dealt with gently, for patience is everything: "Furthermore, you must forgive."

My grandfather's decision "to forgive" pacified him in both good and bad senses of that word. It prevented him from turning his rage into violence. Forgiveness and the discipline of daily, concerted plying of a trade—including the craft of journal writing—were the alternatives to bodily harm, or violent scapegoating, or inchoate anger. And yet his idea of forgiveness may also have rendered him intellectually passive before the complex social forces that placed him where he was. People can be forgiven; systems of power require a different tactic.

Forgiveness could not wholly quell the fears that my grandfather and his family lived with, fears that, according to my grandfather's journal, had more specific contours even than death: fear of invasion of their house, of displacement from their home, and of an estrangement, not "merely" existential, but legally enforced. The house can be invaded at any time:

February 7, 1942. It is Saturday, and it is raining furiously. I have to give my full pay to the gas and electric company if I want to keep it in my home. Yesterday, one of their agents again called on us and tyrannically threatened to shut it off. He didn't go out till my sick wife promised him that she would send me on the next day to pay for it. What is the use of working if you cannot acquire the most necessary things for the existence of your family?

Displacement is imminent:

June 24, 1944. This peaceful spot of Llanerch, no matter how dilapidated it may be, to me is like Eden. Only when I realize that I may be told to vacate whenever the usurper may deem it necessary the feeling is terribly

depressing. Having feelings is very dangerous to mortals. Many head-
aches could be spared if we could get away from being sensitive! Can we?
I doubt it.

And in the wake of 1940s xenophobia, my ancestors' citizen-
ship, even when they are U.S. born, is never certain or is under siege:

Thursday, [?] 30, 1941. Cold, cold and cold! I am a cobbler again.
Inspected my car. My wife an alien! What do you think of that? She has
never left this country, yet born in this city of ours and is considered an
alien! Mrs. Hudson has taken her to the Ardmore Post Office to be finger-
printed. The whole matter is a joke! However it is the law. We are much to
be blamed because we sleep most of the time. We only think but are never
sure. If we would be more alert, we wouldn't be caught in such errors. Once
I thought I was a citizen, but soon I knew different.

February 24, 1942. I have worked a half day. I had to visit the naturaliza-
tion office in regards to my wife. She has lost her citizen's rights by mar-
rying me. And now I have it! Good thing they told me that she doesn't have
to register this time. The office is filled to capacity by people of every age.
I had to wait for two long hours before I could receive that assurance. The
faces of those people showed me a pathetic picture which I shall never erase
from my vision.

But even prior to experiencing official forms of displacement,
my grandfather described himself, like so many other immi-
grants, in estranged terms:

September 27, 1941. The day seems to be a very good one. Business has not changed. Bad as ever. I am dreaming and worrying. I am wondering about what class of a refugee I may be registered as.

The answer to my suffering and to my lacking power is that I was raised in Italy and am living in America and trying to be both I am none.

Will I ever see my little town again? I pray God that I shall!

It is funny, though, that two of the many park guards that were helping motorists get started on their way refused to give me any help. They even refused to lend me a shovel that at that time was not being used.

I am writing as I rest in Gimbel's rest room. The atmosphere is cozy and up to date, but to me? Well I am a stranger!

My grandfather, I am told, was forever unable to look into a camera after the Depression. When someone insisted on taking his picture he looked beyond the camera to some distant point outside it, outside of his body and outside of himself. But he never ceased to look into his garden, and his garden never failed to look back at him. Two stark phrases penned alone onto a page of his journal cut a path into which are planted seeds of self-reflection and hard-won pride: *your large tomato and your rare blooming cactus.* The garden looks back at him, and he looks through it as into a daily mirror: *January 25, 1942. Sunday It is warm Took my family to church Did a little work on shoes Watered my plants Played music with Eleanor and Beatrice Ate [etc].* The garden looks back at him, and he looks through it in wildly shifting metaphors: *Sweet children of mine you make my life a blessedness of fragrance of flowers. / I am truly a failure for all that I have tried has never come to blossom.* He looks through it, and somehow, from some source I can neither find nor grasp, he continuously provides the world with light: *July 5, 1944. The whole day was a pearl. The sky was cloudless. / October 18, 1960. The skies are really enchanting, like a huge lake surrounded by myriads of silver and golden valleys. / October 1, 1941. Got out of bed early. Inspected my garden. The orange tree has blossoms on it.* Who could suspect that surrounding my grandfather's recognition of blossoms are *empty pockets; it is pitch dark / in vain I can find my way to get in / I am broke. Cannot afford car fare to go to school. My store is beginning to get wet / The store is flooded. I cannot fix any shoes. Even the lights are out of commission. It's warm. / Business still a flop. / October 4, 1941. I visited a foreman of the Westinghouse firm, but the result is negative as ever. Again I return to my little dilapidated store, broke, disappointed, and hungry. / October 22, 1941. I am working and starving. This is almost unbelievable in this country of great wealth and democracy. / It is now 4 PM. I have been working steady after lunch from 12:45 and I am tired! Tired yes, tired in every count. The only thought that after having worked so hard I don't have enough to meet my obligations. It makes me shiver! When will I be "man" to earn the amount necessary to live?*

As my grandfather's journals deepen with his age, as he becomes more and more convinced of his failure to make a living and therefore of his failure to make anything or to be "a man," the passages he pens appear as existential runes strewn like inconsequential stones among the flowers: "It is now 8:00 AM. See the constant march of human life. Umbrellas, raincoats, fog, drops of fine mist. / I am the lowest man in intelligence employed and paid and am all by myself in the midst of many human cycles that can admire and understand the human life in every detail as it moves relentlessly like tribes going nowhere." No single person sees any further than another, he seems to say, as we move together into the nothing.

In the middle of summer, the yellow flowers of my grandfather's prickly pear bloom, flowers that are so searingly yellow that the sun seems to have fallen into the earth. My mother's father had years ago added the roaming cactus with its floppy ear-shaped leaves to the slopes that prefaced our backyard gate as well. Each July, after the yellow flowers had made themselves known, my mother tells me, my grandfather would ask my mother if the cactus was bearing fruit—the peculiar pear that gave the plant its name. The question annoyed my mother, who was surprised enough that the cactus bloomed in this nonarid climate, and she'd barely indulge my grandfather's question with a quick and certain no. On the day that my grandfather lay dying, my mother recalls, he asked that question again: "Is there fruit on the prickly pear?" My mother treated the question as she always had, whether she'd checked the plant or not: "No, Daddy. No. There is no fruit." In the days after my grandfather died, my mother, abstractedly inspecting the plant, noticed to her astonishment that for the first time the fruit had appeared.

After my grandfather died, in the process of dismantling with her siblings and mother the house and shoe repair shop, my mother gathered and saved her father's papers. As her own poetry readings coaxed her out of doors, she often read some lines of her father's alongside her own. A declamation had begun, but it was understandably tinged with eulogy. Audience members were moved; painters sketched their visions of my grandfather standing beside my mother when she read; editors compared his work to that of Nazim Hikmet: my mother would try to fulfill the artistic promise that her father thought he'd failed to achieve. My grandfather's dying words rang in her ears: "I am a failure."

CHAPTER 3

Atavism; Or, The Body in Pain

An alarm reminds me / I must forget who I am / If I'm to /
Remember who I am / I return to sleep

FROM ''SHALL I TELL YOU HOW I SPEND MY DAY?''
BY ROSEMARY PETRACCA CAPPELLO

In the past few weeks, I have been having chest pains. I can't
pinpoint the nature of the discomfort—the sensation is new. I
picture tiny muscles, or tiny cushions in the space between my
ribs and lungs, under some inexplicable strain, constricting. Is
this a muscle problem, a breathing problem, or a digestive
problem? I have no idea. I begin to remember the way my father would sit on the living room couch and rub his chest.
Then I begin to worry that I am approaching the age where I
might be inheriting his digestive disorders—it must be a kind

of heartburn I'm experiencing. But, no, I suddenly recall, my father's chest pain was the result of asbestosis, a work-related injury to his lungs for which he was never compensated and for which there is no cure. By the time that he and other victims pursued a lawsuit, the company responsible claimed it was too late. In asbestosis, little fibers scratch away at the delicate lining of a person's airways, forming scar tissue and other manner of obstruction, pain, and inflammation. Asbestosis is not inheritable.

I have been reading my maternal grandfather's journals intensively off and on for the past few months. That could be the source of my pain. For a period of about two years in the early 1960s, still living in poverty, working as the mail clerk at the Philadelphia National Bank in center city, he describes almost daily feeling unwell in the morning but going to work to "fulfill his duty" nevertheless. He sleeps, but barely, because of pains in his chest:

August 7, 1961. Last night I suffered again terrific pains in my chest for many hours and fell asleep for a couple of seconds but thank God again I am able to go to work in spite of my weakness.

February 16, 1961. My head feels heavy and my legs weak. What is the consequence? Age! However the work is very heavy and I cannot explain to myself how I am going through with it. It is the will power and the "Ave Maria" that I devotedly recite in my heart and offer to the reposed in heaven to the souls of my mother and father who have been so dear to me. As I am writing, my head is perspiring very profusely. Perhaps and I hope, it may wash away my unpleasant headaches.

Years and years of injuries have been sustained on the job:

January 29, 1942. It is cold. Today I have punished my body by not eating and have worked with the same steadfastness. Hot chips are burning my hands and face. They also have singed my hair. A hot chip has stuck itself in my face. Believe me, it doesn't tickle!

The chest pains that he begins to experience in the 1960s are no doubt the result of cigarette smoking and possibly of inhaling various toxins in his shoe repair shop. They may be early signs of the lung cancer that will kill him a decade later. Such forms of bodily pain are also not inheritable.

And yet there are ways that we inherit the pain or deformation caused by the material or laboring conditions of our forbears. I am not talking about a genetic disposition that turns up in one's body, but of habits of being that cause one to lie, rest, love, move, speak in one's body in certain ways. Why some members of a family are more prone to observe and imitate the posture of the bodies that early, love them, while others set out for the territories with freshly made up bodies of their own is beyond me. Maybe my chest pains are my own; maybe they are there because I'm identifying with my father and grandfather as a way, however regressive, of trying to understand their lives.

Familial inheritance, I'm convinced, is never a cut-and-dried, unidirectional process. There are qualities that cross generations freely and consciously, but there is also a percentage of unwilled transmission from one generation to the next. There are aspects of heart and attitudes of mind that we wished to have been given but that lay fallow, untaught, unshared. Sometimes what our ancestors don't wish to pass on, good or bad, we most wish to have; many times we miss finding in them what is good for us—so many missed fortunes that we failed to value, resources that we forgot to mine.

Once, in the midst of reading my grandfather's journals, I experienced a burst of strong and pure sobbing. I moved from my study to my bedroom when I felt these loud, uncontrollable tears coming on, but my partner heard me in the next room. She was scared to see me so upset, and thought I was crying out from physical pain. I tried to explain that something happened when I arrived at a particular passage in my grandfather's journal that morning. I'd been reading about his daily struggle, and about his maintenance, in the face of poverty of a genuine belief in the goodness of other people. The kindness and gentleness that persisted in my grandfather's spirit was astonishing. The passage describing my mother and aunt's childhood offering of azaleas secretly picked to give to my great-grandmother as they sang to her released the flood tide in me. The tears enabled me to see more clearly a number of things, not least of which was a sense that I had carried through the years some portion not only of my mother's pain but of my grandfather's. What had been a vague and powerful sensation now met some relief and release.

Poverty afflicts, first and foremost, a person's body. I began to be attuned to the ways in which poverty manifested itself in my mother's body and my mother's work. Certain effects persist even if one experiences "upward mobility," whereas more nebulous forms of pain, some call it psychological pain, are less easily recognized, "treated," or healed. I began to notice how often "teeth" are mentioned in my grandfather's journals. Dental work is a privilege; toothache, mouth pain, loss of teeth— it's a leitmotif in the forties: "My tooth has been extracted. / Another tooth in my family lost. / The thought of losing another tooth that has been so good to me for so many years is bitter. / My little Frances has had two teeth pulled! Do I regret it? And how! Especially when I realize this is due to my poverty! I couldn't give my children the right food and proper medical attention. All my children have some defective teeth." My grandfather rarely records observations about other people in his journals or gives a sense of the trials and tribulations of his intimate relationships. But a passage dated February 22, 1941, regarding his daughter Frances's toothache stands out for the loving, desperate exchange it describes. He wrote it in Italian:

La neve ha incominciato a cadere silenziosa e bella. Fa freddo in questa mia casa. Mia figlia Francesca piange perché vuole le scarpe nuove che le ho promesso. Io la guardo e cerco di confortarla con un mondo di bugie! Terribile esperienza! Una realtà cosí schiacciante mi fa rabbrividire! Più tardi la sento piangere distesa sulla nostra vecchia poltrona. La vedo con le sue guancie coperte di lacrime. "Cosa ti succede?" domando. "Mi fa male una mola," mi fu risposto. La chiamo a me. Le pulisco il dente con tanta delicatezza. Ella mi sorride perché il dente ha cessato di duolerle. O quale delizia veder il suo viso sorridere di più. Io credo ch'essa ha dimenticato le scarpe! Io non ho, ne posso giammai dimenticare! L'esperinze crudeli in cui

traverso ed ho traversato ormai per ben lunghi anni, non mi danno pace!
Tutti i miei bei sogni sono stati infranti come se fossero più fragili dei vetri
all'urto dei venti!

Veder questa mia famiglia cosi in bisognio ed io, legato al lastrico
della tortura, impotente di procurare ciò che é di assoluto bisognio, dispero!
O mio buon Gesù, abbia pietà di me, di questa mia famiglia, di coloro che
sono la cagione dei nostri mali, e di tutta l'umanità! Perdono, perdono mio
Dio!

[The snow has begun to fall silently and beautifully. It is cold in my house.
My daughter Francesca cries because she wants the new shoes that I prom-
ised her. I look at her and try to confront her with a world of lies. Such a ter-
rible experience! A reality so crushing it makes me shudder. Later I see her
again crying, lying on our old armchair. I see her with her cheeks covered
in tears. "What's going on with you?" I ask. "My tooth hurts," I was
answered. I call her to me. I clean her tooth with great care. She smiles at
me because her tooth has stopped hurting her. There was so much delight in
her face that for an instant I thought that she had forgotten the shoes. I had
not, nor could I forget. The cruel experiences I am enduring and those I
have endured for so many long years now, do not give me peace. All of my
beautiful dreams were broken as if they were pieces of glass blown by the
wind.

To see my family in such dire need and me, tied to the star of torture,
impotent to procure what is of absolute need makes me despair. My beauti-
ful Jesus have pity on me, on my family, on those that are the cause of our
pain, and on all of humanity! Pardon, pardon my God!]

Many years later, in the early 1980s, after my mother had
moved to the city alone, with a pittance of alimony from her

divorce from my father ($200 per month), and a college degree earned too late in life, it seemed, for anyone to acknowledge (she was in her mid-forties), with no "prior experience" outside of homemaking and poetry writing to recommend her, she continually found and left secretarial jobs in the public sector. Leaving one such job, she wrote a prose piece that recounts, as I now see it, an unchanged familial condition: joblessness, minimum wage, and toothache remain important themes:

Desperate, I answered an ad in Welcomat and was hired. The ad was for a secretary to two people, a husband and wife non-team. He was a real estate developer and she was a philanthropist. I worked mornings for him and afternoons for her, only he wanted me also mornings and she wanted me afternoons as well. Involvement in this tug of war was maddening, especially when everytime I took my hands off the typewriter she would call out "Rolls, why aren't you typing!" and when my children telephoned she listened in. Meanwhile, the emotional duress of the ages had its effect on my mouth. The dentist told me he'd seen better teeth and gums on a corpse, but he could repair the damage for a figure he'd written on a piece of paper in faint pencil: 7832. I squinted. Strained my eyes. I read it again. That was, $7,832.00. I said doctor, do you know my salary is $10,000 a year? He said if you don't have it done, by next year you'll be holding your teeth in your hands. My boss balked at my absence on the mornings when I went for my dental work, though I returned to work those same days with stitches in my mouth. He complained, though I'd never taken any other sick days, why did I have to have dental work? You have dental work, I told him; why shouldn't I? He said because he after all was a millionaire albeit bankrupt. I only made $10,000 a year and didn't deserve dental work. I'd taken this

job because I was desperate—within a year and a half, a different despera-
tion caused me to leave. I had handed in my 2 weeks' notice, but before the
time was up I couldn't take it anymore. I walked off the job and from my
third floor desk walked down the steps making a speech all the way, fighting
off the bookkeeper who tried to hold me there, out the front door, leaving the
job I was so happy to get, and for three days re-toured historic sites before
becoming a Temp.

I find my mother's physicality much more present in her writing than my grandfather's is in his, and her ability, in spite of a
history of trepidation, to become three times her normal size
in a descent down a staircase is wholly her own. What he would
describe as a defeat, she casts as a triumph. But the body af-
flicted where it takes in nourishment—that remains, as does a
sense that what the world had to offer in the form of work could
never mesh with the shape of their imaginings. A lack of fit.

When they look through their windows, my mother and
her father have similar visions. They observe how other creatures feed themselves and survive. In the 1940s, my grandfather writes:

This morning as I was meditating in my little, yet amiable cage, like a bird
who is waiting for his already late daily meal, I heard my lovely mother's
voice calling: "John, dear, come, come here, quick! I want you to see how
intelligent these lovely little creatures of God are." I instantly upon hear-
ing my mother's voice, broke away from my meditation and ran to the
kitchen window where she was standing, full of smile, looking like a child
at something that he has never seen before. She was pointing where to look
with delight. On the deep snow in our back yard were a few pieces of bread

which she had, as usual, thrown to the little birds. The bread, since the
weather was extremely cold, had become like ice, making it impossible for
the tender beaks to devour. But to my astonishment I saw that one by one,
taking turns, these delicate, pretty, little almost-frozen wrens would lie
on, in order to melt, their heavenly daily bread.

In the 1970s, my mother writes:

I wonder
What the pigeons
Are eating

Their heads bob
Towards earth
And back
Obviously teasing
Something
Out of it

But what?

Not worms
Who have bored
Deep
To survive
The time

Maybe
The pigeons

Are finding
Autumn-discarded
Seeds

Or maybe
They are
Merely
Moistening
Their throats
With ice

Or maybe
They are nibbling
Dirt
Practicing
Eating
While there is
No food

Looking over the books that kept my mother alive, especially a biography of Tolstoy, the life and work of George Sand,
and also of Chi Pai Shih, I notice that the latter has much in
common with my grandfather, and I therefore see my mother's
love of Chi Pai Shih as, in part, a love of finding her father
again. In *Chi Pai Shih*, the painter is described as "a self-taught
artist with a craftsman's background." He makes paintings
whose titles are poems of lucid companions, "Fruit and Wasp,"
"Buffalo and Willow Leaves," "Monk and Frog," "Grapes and
Vine," and he pens lines that have a kinship with my grandfa-

ther's sensibility: "We all know the saying: After three days of wind and four days of rain, can good literature be boiled in the pot and served as food?" "Those who have feelings are prone to be sad." "Setting Fire to My Poems": "I have burnt all my poems, you know, / How can a starving worm produce silk? / I love writing poems but my vocabulary is small; / After so much trouble, why be a laughing stock?"

But I also find my grandfather in less luminous reincarnations. In the early 1980s, after my brother Anthony has dropped out of school, he goes through a period of struggle and transition that begins with an attempt to live on his own. He has commuted to college, and this will be his first foray into self-sufficiency. I visit him in the one-room apartment he has found in a derelict part of Sixty-ninth Street in Upper Darby. When I arrive, I see he has been trying to scrub a set of blinds whose black and yellow stains are beyond cleansing. They lie in a pool of dirty water in the bathtub. On the way out of the bathroom, where my brother has been showing me this project, we both notice a dead mouse, mid-jog, square in the center of the apartment's carpet, that hadn't been there moments before. Preparing dinner, I set a plate atop the stove because there is nowhere else to put it. It bursts into pieces from the heat. I have never seen an object internally combust. It scares me. I apologize profusely—my brother has very few plates. He is not bothered by the breakage, and tells me not to worry about it. These are the only details I remember about my visit, but I also remember that my brother was keeping a journal that he was so eager to share with people that he xeroxed copies of it to distribute. His jobs in this period were various and fleeting:

taxi driver, typewriter salesperson, and forms of volunteer work that he seemed to prefer over everything else. Rereading his journal now, I'd swear my brother had read my grandfather's, but I know that he hasn't: "I don't have a job which pays a living wage. / My love of life is my materialism. My acceptance and sensitivity for people and reaching out to help them is me. Their praise to me is my reward. How to make a living from this? / Spheres of influence are like balloons." My brother craved connection, but the immense remoteness of that stares at me, however kindly, in another passage: "There may be some others out there like me who are starting journals. Advertise to see if there are and compare notes or look into advertising to find them."

When my brothers were boys, my grandfather wrote hopefully of them: "Joe and Anthony now that they see me more often, they are willing to buy me all that I need. Today, Joey said, 'Grandpa, I am going to buy you all new machinery.' That is, for my shop. You see there is a beautiful future for me in store. Most of the conversation took place as he was sitting on my lap eating his lunch." Children can tell, even as babies, what their elders need and desire. For complex and systemic reasons, my brother Joe would not grow up to provide new machinery for my grandfather. He experienced full-blown alienation as a high schooler, stopped performing well in school, although perhaps to his mind and that of the neighborhood he succeeded by losing the weight that was the bane of his existence—he'd no longer be mocked as fat, but desired for his slender body. He had been accepted to the Berklee School of Music, but at the last minute, announced he was not going.

Years later, he explains to me that he was afraid he'd be alone. As a single parent trying to make a living as a musician, he, too, lives in near poverty. For ten years, he works as a roofer, and he complains about the backbreaking, finger-crippling, and mind-numbing grind of his job. He has periodic gigs that reawaken his interest in composing, but mostly he suffers long bouts of unemployment that result in my niece and nephew's receiving substandard medical care, food, educational privileges, and child care. Eventually he lives on the public assistance that my grandfather eschewed, but that program enables him, now nearing age forty, to enter university, where he is continually recognized for his newfound talents as a computer programmer and budding physicist. He has never gotten counseling for the years of my father's abuse of him, and it shows.

My own desire for my family is no less ambitious than my brother's was as a child. I decide that my family needs for its enigmas—its self-imposed secrets and fears—to be interpreted, so that they might float off like balloons, no longer burdens but light and lambent globes. When I look in the direction of my family, what I hope to find in them are images: dreams appear as bits of glass blown by wind; a father cleans, delicately, the tooth that pains his daughter; birds melt their frozen bread with the warmth of their small bodies; spheres of influence are like balloons. What I want to learn from my family is the ability to see—as my grandfather put it, *veder più meglio, più lontano*, "to see better, farther."

That I have "left" the working class does not mean that I am not heir to familial repetitions. I did not rise above and beyond some form of familial ailment. I love deeply, speak boldly, rest restlessly, move uncertainly. Now I wonder if my early and developing ability to impersonate is in part what led me out. When I was no more than three years old, I came to impersonate a character whom Jackie Gleason had created, a drunken bartender named Crazy Googenheim whom I had seen on TV. I remember being asked on numerous occasions to perform my imitation at family gatherings. I would squash my face into a puddinglike pose, screw up and wet my little mouth, and then speak the two lines of dialog I remembered: "Hellooooo Joe." "Hellooooo Mr. Donahee, hee, hee, hee." Each "hee" demanded a higher pitch. My audience would be reduced to convulsive laughter. As I got older, other characters were added to my repertoire: Julia Child, Rex Reed, Minnie Pearl, Curly from the Three Stooges, to name a few. My friends tried to convince me that there was a future for me as a comedian. On Sunday afternoons as a teenager, I watched *Soul Train* and movies with Fred Astaire. When I danced with friends at the local "sock hops," I was told I danced "like a black person." Later in life, dancing with exhibitionistic abandon, ballroom-style with my partner, I'm asked in awe where I learned to dance. "By watching Fred Astaire," I unabashedly announce. Being a good imitator requires a highly developed visual sense—you need to watch for details—and a degree of impressionability.

I am a receptor. Because I tend to reject nothing, I am often overwhelmed. The positive upshot of this condition is that I have learned from my family what they didn't expect me to learn. And I have learned from them what I wanted to learn but what may not have been explicitly given—myriad creative ways of dealing with loss.

"None could have had ever me believe that I would become what I am now," my grandfather wrote. Whether this referred to a downward or upward spiral, the line implies a lack of fit. For marginal peoples, x does *not* yield y. This is what could not be exposed to the outside world; this was the unutterable news: John Petracca had not become what he had imagined he could be. John Petracca could not fulfill the promise that life in the United States was supposed to have made possible. Shame was illumined in the immigrant household, and shame has a tendency to attach to and fuel fear.

Like my grandfather, I wish to resist determinism, but differently so. I have decided, for example, that I am reluctant to work with conventional narrative because my life, I, did not conform to the narrative meant for me. I was not supposed to get from "there" to "here." Turning to the next generation, I listen for alternative endings. I have sent my niece Ilia a video of the Hollywood film version of *Guys and Dolls*. She is performing in her school's version of it (she's twelve), and I think she will like to see the film. I remark on how long the film turns out to be; she agrees. She tells me she enjoyed singing along with the songs, and that, at a certain point, singing alongside the voice and words she knew so well, her voice grew softer, and then she fell asleep. My nephew (he's ten) tells me of a book he's reading. It's called *Silver Wings*. He's sure I don't know it. What he loves about this book is that it never ends. He keeps remarking this. Then he clarifies: the book comes with four different endings depending on how the reader solves its characters' conflicts—a journey they are attempting on an airplane. "It says The End, The End, The End, The End, four times in four different places," my nephew says. "It's cool." I wish . . . to learn from them.

TWO

CHAPTER 4

All Things Swim and Glitter

If you want to step into the open space, be sure of every corner.

FROM THE JOURNAL OF JOHN PETRACCA

A soft brown wool jumper with a knoblike hip-high button. This was my mother's riding outfit, or so I imagined it as a pre-schooler. My mother's brown jumper signified to me an excursion, an outing, a walk that we would make together. My mother didn't drive. My mother loved to walk. My mother addressed me as her "sidekick": "Are you my sidekick?" "Would my sidekick like to join me in a walk?" "Shall my sidekick and I go find a book in the library?" The word jingled in my pants cuffs, my sleeves, my shoes. I loved the way it tickled me. The word "sidekick" made me think of a friendly elf who walked alongside one's more orderly self. He kicked up his heels while your other self, the self that people could see, walked a stiff and

59

dignified straight line. As sidekick, I was my mother's laughing, skipping companion. Lest I should lose the word, its happy feeling, I tethered it to the toy that then became the favorite miniature vehicle in my Matchbox Car collection: the motorcycle and sidecar. When my mother addressed me as her sidekick, I pictured her revving up the engine of her cycle with me securely stowed, scarf riding the wind, in her sidecar as we readied ourselves to roam the countryside and seek out adventure.

A walk to the library was always prefaced with this scene: I stand in the doorway of my mother's bedroom and watch her watching herself in the mirror as she combs her hair. She sings. Songs I can't now remember. Songs about sidekicks. I materialize in my mother's voice. I picture myself in her image. I traverse time in a light-year—the swift, deep, and magical space between the image of myself as a four-year-old girl and the image of myself as my mother who is a thirty-year-old woman. My mother is singing. And now we are walking. My mother is singing and walking. All things swim and glitter. If I choose to walk to the right, she puts me back in my sidecar to the left— she lets me know she's protecting me from the traffic of the semi-busy highway called Lansdowne Avenue. One hand is looped into my mother's; the other hand carries a rather impractical yellow basket from some former Easter that I insist on using to carry my books. I try to make my shoes mimic the sound of my mother's on the pavement—the sound of a benign giant stepping gently yet confidently, grinding silt underfoot.

The Darby Library appears on the horizon like an oasis. All things swim and glitter. It was the physical details of the library itself that led me to love what one does in the library—read books. I loved that a rose window (though I didn't know to call it that) emblazoned the front; that Abraham Lincoln looked like a good, kind man in the photograph; that the staircase that led from the children's to the adult section was like nothing I knew, winding, gyring, steep and narrow; that you could count on the librarian, Mrs. Valutis, knowing you, and on quiet, comforting quiet.

Whether fairies danced in a mote of light or rain tapped at the windowsill on the ground floor, no matter the weather, I usually made two kinds of choices: one book from the *Curious George* series, and a poetry book, my favorite being *A Child's Garden of Verses*. Back home, my mother read these books to me, while I studied the details of the pictures until I found myself in them. I felt an unusual kinship with Curious George.

Now I walk in front of my mother as we climb the staircase to the adult section. The staircase takes more than one sharp turn and narrows as it climbs. My mother chooses fat books for herself, especially biographies, some of which she will eventually have to purchase and reread because they come to mean so much to her. Some children remember and learn from their mother application to a craft: they watch her articulate a pattern, prepare food, or at the very least they learn to sew a button on or to make a bed. I learned neither a literal nor metaphoric stitch of "homemaking" from my mother. Daily and intently, I watched, rather, the work of my mother's reading, and I noted how this work far outweighed any other in keeping her alive. I am most aware of the life of my mother's desire when she is with her books—her books are speaking to her, she is in conversation with their authors, they are meeting a hunger and opening a space for her to listen for the sound of her own voice.

My mother's books are squeezed alongside her desk and typewriter in a corner of the dining room. The space in my friends' houses is stark by comparison: one friend's mother keeps the blinds eternally drawn, and the air conditioner—one of the few in the neighborhood—seems to chill the house year-round; another friend's mother vacuums the wall-to-wall carpeting every day all day. Not a stitch of paper can be found there, and neither home seems to own a book outside of the Bible. My friends like my mother and her lively, because cluttered, house. My friends enjoy my mother because she lends them her books and lets them consult her homespun library for school projects.

The heady silence of the adult section of the library will soon be broken by the light of my mother's exuberant smile and by the conversation she encourages to ripple and unfold between her and the otherwise serious, silent Mrs. Valutis. At the end of the conversation—a conversation about books and flowers—Mrs. Valutis will look at me the way the bank tellers do before bestowing their free lollipops—wistfully, smilingly, as though I remind them of something they want. All things swim and glitter. In place of a sweet, Mrs. Valutis gives me a book—usually whatever book my mother has special-ordered for herself for that week. "Is there room in your basket for another book?" she asks. "You can never have too many," she says, and I watch my books multiply like colored eggs.

In the descent down the highly pitched staircase, I walk with my mother behind me. She instructs me to hold onto the railing. I won't really observe until I'm an adult that, confronted with certain staircases, my mother needs another person to walk in front of her. Midway down the stairs, a narrow window looms to the right. I've bounded to the bottom, but my mother's steps have ceased to follow me. "Wait!" she says. "Wait!" And my mother seems to whimper and breathe heavily, to pace, if that's possible, from one side of a single narrow step to the other. She can't walk up the steps; she can't walk down the steps. She appears to be spinning, as though the staircase has become a spinning ball poised on the nose of a seal, and my mother is being made to walk on the surface of the ball. Or it's as though the steps have become a room, a room that defies the shape of things as she knows them, a room where surfaces repel and clouds are solid, a room in which she is forced to grope. All things swim and glitter.

My mother suffered in those years from migraines, the kind that take a person to bed and spit her out the other side of her body in a few days time. Even though her body was probably hypersensitized in those episodes, she would let me stroke her head. I would stroke her head and pray: "Dear God, please make Mommy's headache go away." My mother always made me feel as though my magic touch had cured her. My hand could not reach my mother's forehead on the stairs. This was a different trouble. It was a pantomime, a charade I must interpret. It was all body and no words. My making a life of reading has, I know, everything to do with the pleasure and horror of trips with my mother to the Darby Library. It's as much about refuge as it is about unbearable confrontation.

In the 1940s, my mother stands at the bottom of the staircase in her family's home and can do nothing but watch as her grandmother crawls up the steps. Her father's mother, a second mother to her, Josephine Conte was a hardworking woman whose suffering was immense, whose frame was tiny, whose love was bountiful, but who would accept no sympathy. In the last decade of her life, Josephine Conte endured crippling arthritis. Each night was a trial, my mother told me, since her grandmother would not allow anyone to help her crippled self climb the stairs. She'd crawl. Each night she crawled up the staircase to bed. Grandmother Josephine, who was as vulnerable and indomitable as life itself, who spoke a foreign language, who nevertheless enjoyed a good Hollywood Western, whose eyes spoke worlds to my mother, who called my mother *bella* and who told her in a language of their making that my mother, of all the grandchildren, looked most truly like a Neapolitan, looked most like all of the children whom my great-grandmother lost to childhood illnesses, poor living conditions, rabid dogs, fear, and harm—Josephine Conte should have let my mother carry her up the stairs.

In the 1960s, I stand at the bottom of a staircase. I watch my mother dangle there. The hem of my mother's longing is caught on the stair, and I cannot release it to retrieve her. I only know this should not be happening to my mother—my mother who loves to walk, who walks and sings, who shields me from the accidents that might occur, who heals me from those that do, who lets me carry my books in a basket, whose slender fingers comb my slender hairs, whose adamant hands arrange flowers in a blue vase, who carries her books like a cup of roses to the librarian's desk, who helps to make the librarian's day. All things swim and glitter. Here she is vexed; she is irresolute. My mother's confusion on the library stairs is a mark of profound indecision: should she turn backward to her grandmother, now deceased, who would not let her demonstrate her love to her, or move forward in her body, into the present, down or up staircases, as a woman who has learned to carry herself? As a mother who might still occasionally carry me?

Memory catches and memory cuts. Memory attaches and memory subtracts. All things swim and glitter. I have no memory whatsoever of the walk home from the library. Memory rearranges. On a recent visit to my father's house in Darby, I decided to make a return trip by foot to the Darby Library to see if being in its presence again could conjure aspects and details of its power in my life that I had forgotten. While in childhood the walk had stretched out for several pleasant miles, while space from that vantage was magnified, I now saw with great surprise that the trip from Concord Road to the Darby Library was a few quick, short blocks. Maybe children know and agoraphobes wish to remember that space does not stand still but is ever rolling, space is not the square feet that we measure and master in our boots but the water in which we swim and glitter.

When I told my mother that I was making a return trip to the Darby Library to see what I could see there, she said she wished she could come with me. Then she looked happily reflective, and said: "I always loved the staircase there." I didn't contradict her; nor did I understand. To understand might require an act of willed detachment, to comprehend is to willingly let go. My mode is more one of apprehension: 1. to take hold of; 2. to grasp; 3. to fear; 4. to understand, a little.

> *January 21, 1946.* Va o mio bel pensiero in ogni dove poiché lo spazio è senza limiti. *[Go! My good thoughts wherever you please; after all, space has no limits.]*
>
> FROM THE JOURNAL OF JOHN PETRACCA

Both my grandfather and my mother found various forms, in solitude and community, for expressing the politics of their daily lives. My grandfather was a musician and sculptor who taught me to play mandolin, and my grandmother to play guitar. He also helped to found a mandolin and guitar society. My mother organized poetry readings, edited a poetry journal of her own creation in Philadelphia for many years, and most recently has become a self-taught painter of figures of mandala-like proportion named for the sound in her ear when she suffered a severe ear infection (*Sound*), memories of her own mother's unusual though seasonal art (*Mother's Palm 2*), and daily political struggles: during Lorena Bobbitt's trial, she made a canvas of permanent rose and deep turquoise (*Woman Rising*). But the form that persists even as it takes different shapes across three generations in my family is the letter, sent or unsent. While waiting for leaves or flowers to line the trees, my grandfather and mother seem to have created letters like lines strung with lanterns reaching toward some other. Now in the days of electronic mail, one friend writes, "You are one of my few (only?) e-mail correspondents who write real letters and talk about difficult things naturally on the net," and letters consistently become the bases of or impetus behind my poems. I have written poems using excerpts from letters received when the words asked to be shared with others or threatened to uplift themselves off the page. Poems write themselves in lieu of letters or because of the impossibility of sending a letter. If I cannot write you a letter, let me find a poem.

My family's letters begin in a language I cannot read; they leave a strong scent linked to a memory not my own but that seems to reside in my body nonetheless. In their better moods, they leave traces of the work they did of love, a form of saving, well done. It is odd to have so many of my grandfather's unsent letters—I don't want to wear them as keepsakes around my neck, nor can I take up the thread, Emily Dickinson–style, and bind them into a book well-kept but drafty. A letter conjures a listener, but does it need to be sent and received to fulfill its promise? Perhaps my grandfather saved rather than sent so many of his letters because he didn't trust his command of the language, or the worthiness of his love. Perhaps he was distracted by a customer entering the store, or the completion of some other task prevented him from completing the circle that a letter inscribes. My mother guides my fingers over the raised marks and impressions made from where the words began:

LETTERS
written in Italian
by a young man to a
teenage American girl
who couldn't understand them
she'd ask her stepmother to
translate them,
but she wouldn't

Now, the pages are thin
and brittle
here and there, what once were real
violets
he placed within a page are
purple marks
what once were
words,
black blurs
A fragile art.

My grandfather keeps a dictionary on the dining room table and reads, longs to write, in English. I am a child, so I give him a gift that I would enjoy—a box of chocolate-covered cherries. He gives me my first lesson in poetry in the form of a thank-you letter:

Dear Mimi:

I am writing a few phrases to thank you for your delicious and most welcome cherry gift. Due to the stubbornness of age, my teeth are unwilling to chew such sweetness, and I am usually forced to look and not enjoy such delicacy. But now, I am going to dissolve the candies in my coffee, making a chocolate drink adorned with pretty cherries.

Over the years, he has corresponded with Irving, a man who had spoken of suicide during the Depression and who credited my grandfather's "homespun philosophy" with saving him:

Dear Irving:

I am answering your letter while pacing up and down the sunny side of the yard of my cozy home. The weather is so marvelous after the zero period of a few days ago that I am without an overcoat. Imagine such a change! It seems impossible, yet it is true. This teaches us not to despair, for good days are always in store for us all.

As he writes these lines, his daughter Josephine is confined to a darkened room with an illness called St. Vitus' dance, and the mortgage company has threatened foreclosure. Years after, Irving has died, so my grandfather writes to his wife:

Dear Mrs. Peterson:

How are you? your children? your condition? Please write and let us know all. It may do you good to write to us and vice versa.

I would love to write to you but I don't know if you would enjoy my way of writing as your late husband did. If you would, I would be only glad to write now and then as I did to Irving. I am trying to translate a favorite

book of mine from an Italian poet, and if you care I could send you part by
part as I progress.

Please accept the enclosed dollar and buy some ice cream for your little
ones, and of course, a cone for you, too.

We hope you are well and wish you a brighter future.

In the late 1940s, two of my aunts, the two eldest daughters, entered a semi-cloistered convent together. My grandfather was devastated by their absence, but my grandmother refused to let him send them the letters he wrote to them—they were too sad. Now my mother, age fourteen, took up the pen, soon to learn in an odd combination of prohibition and release, refusal and reception, that the mother superior would read all letters before the sisters saw them and black out lines where she saw fit. Enchanted by my mother's teenage accounts of the latest family news, the mother superior read her letters to the entire convent community while secretly preparing a place for her among them when she came of age. My mother never became the convent scribe or church's muse, but this almost accidental encouragement launched an identity in letters, and she later went so far as to compose feminist sermons for a progressive parish priest.

By the time my mother was the age I am as I write this, in her late thirties, she had borne three children and an unresponsive, often violent husband. More a hippie than a happy homemaker—the walls in our house were painted mandarin orange and cobalt blue—my mother nevertheless struggled daily as so many women still do, with the oppressive nature of domestic Law. When fear and depression literally kept her from leaving the house, she sent out lifelines in the form of letters, so many match stems, sometimes blazing, sometimes quickly spent, in the dark.

In 1958 she won a letter-writing contest sponsored by a Philadelphia radio station on the topic of a woman who had become a member of Congress (the prize was an Osterizer that is now a splendid objet d'art); she began to treat the newspaper as a letter begging for response. She invited public figures whose work spoke to her into our working-class living room: Salvador Dali and Ingmar Bergman didn't reply, but Sam Levenson and Lady Bird Johnson did. When a local radio station featured a discussion of whether priests should be able to marry as a cure for loneliness, she wrote a long letter to one of the discussants—a monsignor who was also a newspaper editor—about the great periods of loneliness endured in fifteen years of marriage to the wrong person, and she told stories that her female neighbors had told her of frequent loneliness and abuse. The monsignor published the piece on the front page of his paper and solicited subsequent articles on timely issues from my mother for a number of years. Meanwhile, my mother had started to correspond with a new friend through the mail—a Californian woman poet, who only coincidentally suffered as well from agoraphobia and whose poetry was claiming attention on the West Coast. My mother and Annie have written each other letters—whatever, whenever, in the mood or out of the mood, never having to wait for the other to write before putting the next missive in the mail. They have told each other their daily lives for the past twenty years and, I'm convinced, on some level cured each other of despair, many a time saved each other through letters from drowning.

While composing this, I received the shocking news via an alumni publication that a man who was dear to me as an undergraduate was killed in a bicycling accident. That news led me to return to the sporadic communication we had maintained through letters. I dug through mounds of mail packed away in my cellar for a bit of Tom's spirit and voice, his tendency toward old yellow-lined legal-sized paper and a black fountain pen. While reading, I found the following commentary on letter writing and, of all things, the presence of my *mother's* letter-writing practice in that past:

It's wonderful to hear from you; I knew I could rely on you to send me a fat envelope bursting with news and ideas, not to mention poetry. Though I didn't quite expect such a hefty package, not after so many years. My friends have mostly joined the telephone fraternity and find it difficult to master the energy to write when it's so easy to call. Only a few destitute friends out in California for whom a cross-country phone call is still a monetary indulgence continue to correspond by mail. Yet, I would always prefer a letter to a phone call. From past experience, I know that the Cappello family, for one, will continue to prevent the postman from becoming an anachronism; I still remember receiving a note from your mother before, if I recall correctly, we had ever become acquainted.

My mother, it now occurred to me, perhaps was wrong to have called letter writing a "fragile art" in her poem. My memory of

Tom would indeed have been fragile if *not* for this bundle of letters, the impress of his mind's body meandering, brooklike, over, around, and through each distinct formation of the alphabet. And *her* letter to him, as from a stranger, was one part of a pulse in him.

If letter writing is really a fragile art, that's only because, as my family has demonstrated to me, the medium has to contain unspeakable truths and inappropriate yearnings other narrative options seem unable to admit. My immigrant heritage is marked by inappropriateness, delegitimized sound, call it the noise of my grandfather's desire to make a living crafting shoes, of my mother's desire to be accounted for as a woman, of my desire to love other women, of our collective desire to be writers in an American culture that stifles the imagination of difference and that refuses artistic practice as a place around which the mind and heart might rally.

Now I try to understand the pathological sense of loss (in the form of depression) and fear (in the form of phobia) that characterizes my ethnic heritage: the manifest calls whose response was the letter. I can locate the source of disjunction in the immigrant status, the initial anomie of being out of place; but that sense of separation may have only expanded in proportion to my grandfather's un-macho ways and my mother's unladylike tendency to tell it like it is—this in the light of the patriarchal history of Mediterranean culture aided and abetted by the misogynist spirituality of the Catholic Church.

My mother is "cured" now—when writing fails, she paints; when painting fails, she dances; when dancing fails, she remembers her parents; when memory fails, she takes long walks. My mother has filled her closets with color; she has fought the dragon fear and won. Before my mother left the church, left my father, got a college degree, moved to the city where she found, in the arts community, an outdoors that could accommodate her largeness of spirit, before she moved to the city where she found a wise and compassionate analyst who was not afraid to help her, she wrote letters. And this history of uneasiness tempered by lives of letters with which I was surrounded growing up has made me aware of how little is actually said or shared about the labors and machinations of our inner lives in a culture dominated by the confessional modes of the Talk, Talk, Talk Show. Letters may be precisely the place where a dislocation of what's come to be thought of as the "personal" can truly occur.

My mother is "cured" now . . . but I still find it hard to treat agoraphobia with a sense of humor. A recent TV guide helps me with the description of a movie about an agoraphobic who gets a roommate to help her with her rent. The roommate comes complete with a man who is not her brother (as assumed) but her lover who is also a murderer. Now the agoraphobic isn't sure whether to be more frightened by the murderer or by the prospect of going out. When I tell a friend who is a Beckettian about my mother's one-time inability to get past the three steps that marked the front of our house, she explains that Beckett would use the condition to create a character stuck on the steps, unable to tell whether there are one, two, or three steps to be mastered, for it would depend on where you're standing to know where to begin.

Depression and agoraphobia are not failings but responses, conditions, ways of saying. When my mother painted the walls of our cramped home orange and blue, she was trying to let enter the sun, the moon. As a child, I let the blue surround me in tidal comfort as I tried to fall asleep. But I worried about my mother, and I worried about myself if someday she should disappear forever into that sadness. It's past midnight, and I still can't sleep . . . until I hear the tiny tick of the gas stove, and smell coffee percolating. Now I know my mother's pen is moving across the page: my mother writes the letter that I dream. Like a walk in the garden, it is not a grand gesture, but it is profound. The letter means that someone else is walking with her, that she will be there in the morning, that I can sleep.

CHAPTER 5

Cut Curls in a Box

Children are afraid in the dark because in the dark they cannot see the person they love.

SIGMUND FREUD,
THREE ESSAYS ON THE THEORY OF SEXUALITY

To know what is in store for us in our life is not to be known till we embark in the open fields away from our parents. In the open space is our future, but sad to say we do paddle our canoe in a river between illusion and disillusion.

FROM THE JOURNAL OF JOHN PETRACCA

I awake one day to paper dolls. Cut-outs of a blonde girl's tennis outfit, sunsuit, school uniform. This girl has folk wear—a plaid kilt, beaded moccasins, a white fur hat for her treks in the Caucacuses, blue overalls for her stint on the farm. I can't place her. She's from everywhere and nowhere, but no matter what suit I choose for her, she maintains the same determined smile. This paper doll has ruddy cheeks, fat on her imperceptible bones, and freckles. Her face tells me she agrees to everything; she is never ornery, never "contrary," never "horrid" like the little girl there was once, "There once was a girl who had a little curl," like me, "right in the middle of her forehead." If my paper doll could speak, she'd probably say, "Yah!" like the robotically cheerful Katie, "the farmer's daughter," on TV.

Occasionally when I was afraid to go to sleep as a child, I would ask my mother to sleep with me. Once my mother had to tear me, finger by finger, off my brother's bed. I kicked and screamed, "Why am I the only one who has to sleep alone?" My parents slept together; my brothers shared a bedroom; but I, presumably privileged, slept in another cubicle of our row home. My mother, who was raised in poverty and shared a bed out of necessity with her parents and her siblings, couldn't entirely sympathize with my wish; nevertheless, once or twice my mother agreed to share my bed with me. I think what happened was that she planned to stay only until I fell asleep, intending to creep quietly back to her room, because in the morning she'd still be fully dressed, even aproned, asleep in the opposite direction from me at the foot of my bed. Nothing delighted me more than to find my mother with me in the morning, though I also stemmed that pleasure by telling myself that she really hadn't slept well and would suffer for it as she tried to do her housework the next day.

On the night before the morning of the paper dolls, my sickness pulled me unto it and into sleep even though I kept looking back to where my mother stood. I was groggy when she showed me the thick blur of a booklet that the pieces of the paper doll's wardrobe were laid out in, and I remember how excited my mother was herself with the gift: paper dolls, she explained, had been among her favorite playthings as a child. In the morning, she presented me with the doll's intricate wardrobe, now neatly extracted from the pages of the book, stacked, arranged by type—outer, under, folk, school, and play—and paper-clipped together. My mother had stayed up a better part of the night cutting out the clothes. This, to me, was almost as good as having her sleep in my bed.

I had seen my mother wield the heavy wooden garden shears to shape her grandfather's hedge before our house, but I did not know until then of her more delicate abilities as a surgeon. Awaking to my paper dolls, I was released from the previous night's fever as though my mother, in extracting the clothes from their pages, had excised a hurt and exorcised my illness. Suffused with joy at the neat pile of miniature clothes, I did not question the fact that there was nothing left for me to cut. As I saw it, my mother had done the work so I could enjoy the play. I also knew that though I owned my own pink-handled pair of scissors, I had not been trusted with them ever since, bathing in the otherworldly glow of the TV set one evening, I had applied the scissors unconsciously to my four-year-old curls. My mother's voice had come to me at first as through a paper telephone, so close to my ear and yet so thoroughly inaudible—all I could make out was a muffled thrum as of paper brushing against flesh, and the feel of the actual scissors clipping my hair was like a deeply satisfying munch. Then, as though she'd leapt across several senses, my mother squeezed my wrist—I felt it now—to compel my fingers to release the scissors. She looked at me with horror and picked up the curls as though they were the fragments of a once whole family heirloom. I pouted, then screamed, uncertain of how what felt so good in the doing could mean something so wrong.

Not those curls but some others of mine from the occasion of a more skillful cutting were kept by my mother in a thin long white box, a box that might have held a silken pair of gloves now transformed into a tiny coffin for my silken curls. As a preteen I would sometimes stumble upon the box marked "Mary's curls" while searching for a Magic Marker in the drawer to the hutch. I'd lift the lid slowly to confront what looked like the body of a dead baby animal that once was me, that had some affiliation with me, that had my name. Presumably the neighborhood hairdresser who couldn't bear to sweep and trash the curls she'd cut from my head insisted tearfully that my mother take them home.

Receiving something in the morning that materialized while one slept had the cachet of the mystery of Christmas presents. But there was more than a Hallmark stamp to the memory of the gift of paper dolls for me because of my awareness of the importance of nighttime for my mother, of the way in which she inhabited the night. Sometimes my mother, like her mother, suffered from insomnia. My grandmother mostly slept sitting up, or at the movies, or at the kitchen table before a vase of peonies she had just arranged. Even as I slept, I could often sense my mother moving about in the light that emanated from the base of the stairs, a thick but clear caramel-colored light, in the deepest darkest middle of the night. Other times, there was just the sense that nighttime was *her* time—her time to think, to write, to dream.

The capacity of my mother to live a different, alert, and vital life at night was recognized by the doctor at the nearby hospital who was treating me for a head injury when I was seven years old. I had been engaged in the fearless repetition of a series of shrieking plunges from the high diving board of the local public swim club into the waters below. My father had told me it was time to go home. I told him that I just wanted to go off the high dive one more time. At the top step, I slipped and fell backward onto cement. As an adult, I am able to retrace the memory back to watching my foot slip between the steps. And to what I said as I came back into consciousness: "Is it a dream, or is it real?" But I fail to remember the way my father reacted. He witnessed the fall, and ran to gather me up. And then, according to my mother, my father went hysterical as though he experienced a kind of break. He screamed and screamed about the blood, "Where was all of the blood coming from!?" but there was no blood, or at least not until I arrived at the hospital, where a slender stream of blood trickled out of my ear. Because of the severity of the concussion, I was expected to stay overnight in the hospital for care and observation. My mother did not want me to stay in the hospital alone, but the doctor explained it would be impossible to release me since someone would have to wake me up every hour on the hour, then ask me a series of questions to be sure I hadn't experienced brain damage. My mother convinced the doctor that she would have no trouble staying up all night to carry out this task, and as my father, still in shock, stunned and drained by the sight of the accident, carried me through the front door of our home and then retreated to bed, my mother put the coffee on.

I don't know what was more traumatizing—the actual fall, loss of and return to consciousness or that night of being awakened, my head pounding with a start into the whisper of my mother's arousal, of being asked my name, to spell it, to identify the faces before me of my mother and brothers, to make two plus two come out to four and three plus three to six. For the first few hours, my brothers accompanied my mother with their own impish questions, but further into the night, the beginning of each hour was filled only with my mother's face asking me to tell her who I was. I must have thought it a cruel trick, a ghoulish form of torture that my family was asking me to come out of sleep and into an awareness of my bruises at the same time that they posed questions to me whose answers were as plain as day. My mother tells me that I was angry with them all, that I reluctantly answered the questions correctly even as I kept asking in return *why* they were asking me to tell them what we all already knew. I don't know whether it would have been worse to have been awakened by a stranger to the question of my identity in a hospital room or to be awakened by my mother feeding me strange questions in familiar quarters.

Recovery and return to school didn't diminish the uncanny feeling left in the wake of my accident and its treatment. I remember being interrogated by the school nurse, and other lay authorities of whom I was fond suddenly treated me as someone other than myself. I felt fine; I felt no different than before, but the faces I met saw or expected something different when they looked at me, and this annoyed, confused and scared me. I remember knowing I was finally in the clear, that the veil had lifted, when I heard the school nurse tell my mother one day: "She's the same wonderful little Mary. Nothing has changed." But so much had changed. In my return to school, I had been chanting, "I'm here. Hello. It's me." And for a spell, I was answered with, "But *are* you?" I had experienced for the first time in a profound or cognizant way the exile of illness, and I hated the way the people around me made me feel, as though I didn't know who I was while they remained "familiar."

The only really splendid memory I have of those first few months of the return to school occurs in art class. The project entails scissors, orange and black construction paper (it's autumn) cut into tiny squares, and the application of the confetti to a drawing I have made of a Pilgrim who is mostly hat and not much else. Usually in art class I struggle with the discrepancy between the picture that I make and the picture in my head, but the making of the mosaic hat has the opposite effect: in this case, the reality edges up to the dream, and the act of cutting and pasting reveals a picture I didn't know was there. I enjoy watching each square contribute to the development of the whole, a whole I could never have anticipated as the tip of my index finger dots each square with Elmer's, places it carefully alongside its fellow square, and calculates the geometry required to fit the squares into the edges of the blunt triangular hat. The addition of square to square gives the effect of something woven until it looks like the hat has pockets, invisible chambers, valleys where I have pressed harder on a square, hills where I've used too large a bubble of glue. For some reason, I begin to be compelled to kiss each square before I apply it. Because I associate the Pilgrims with the ocean, a buckle, and a rock, I choose to make gray and blue confetti in addition to the autumn colors for the time of year. The teacher, making his rounds, comments on the novel interplay of color, but then he asks me where my Pilgrim's body has gone. Mesmerized by the cutting of more squares, I pretend not to hear his question: Can't he see that the hat is as large as a stomach, that the body is in the hat? Doesn't he know that it is easier to spell my name in English, H-A-T, than in Italian, C-A-P-P-E-L-L-O, in the middle of the night? Doesn't he know that I pretend not to hear now when people ask me stupid questions?

Paper dolls, a period of anomie, cut curls in a box: I don't know if these pieces of my past lined up to form a particular week or season or year, but they are the elements that coalesce for me now as backdrop, as padding, as gauze applied to the wound of what I hope to write of but what is so hard to approach: fear. Memories of my mother's incomprehensible fear; the situation of my own fears; the occasional feeling that nine-tenths of any psyche is composed of fear. Childhood fear, adult fear, private, public, acceptable, and unacceptable fear, unutterable fear, nameless fear, immobilizing fear. Shame and fear. Fear of fear. The gulf between my mother's fierceness, my mother's courage, and my mother's fear. The female members of my family were some of the strongest, fiercest women I have known, but they also appear in my memory frozen on the hither side of uncrossable lines, stricken with fears all out of synch with the patterns their sure and nimble feet have made.

The women in my family managed myriad forms of trauma in their lifetimes, and they were consummate wielders of the word: they loved to talk, and people loved them for the way they listened; they looked you in the eye; they sang out, they spoke out, they cried out. But their powers—magical, loving, creative—seemed to vanish or be vanquished at the threshold of the physical world. Stairways, tunnels, bridges, and cars; escalators, elevators, ladders, and planes; bicycles and trains—all those things that men had made as means of transport through the world those same men had built—terrorized them, rejected them, fooled their bodies into thinking they were weak. And yet there had been instances in both private and public worlds when my mother, whose fears I must have been most acutely aware of, became larger than any outmoded worn-down image of femininity, instances when men felt the full force and presence of her physical body.

Fear's yawp, fear's buzz, fear's devilish grin, fear's thin or thick skin. Fear's exuberance, the exhilarating trigger of fear, the exhausting nature of fear. Fear that others excite in us, fear that is our inheritance, fear that has a basis in physical harm, fear that the body remembers but the mind forgot. Fear that certain people in our lives help us to ride and release.

The poignant absurdity of fear, the grief that fear hides, the longing that fear expresses, the sadness that is fear.

I wasn't allowed to use the scissors because I had once used them wrongly to cut my own hair. But this wasn't the only reason. A fear that was my mother's surrounded scissors. Without her having told me until I was an adult, I knew, I always knew, of the event that left the horrific impression on scissors: that her nearest sister, Frances, who suffered from undiagnosed mental disorders all of her life, had, when they were children, gone at my mother's eye with a pair of scissors. My mother remembered most the sweat that appeared in beads on her sister's brow just before she landed the gash on my mother's face. Maybe my mothers's sister's violence interrupted my mother's quiet play with paper dolls as rainy day consolation. Each careful snip of paper doll clothes for me was meant to seal that wound. To use the scissors to repair, to make, to complete the afternoon as it was meant to be, to cut the memory of her sister's use of scissors out of her life. I ever approached scissors with trepidation.

Like most children, I was afraid of what lived under my bed, and of being sucked down the drain along with the suds whenever my mother washed my hair; unlike most children, I was afraid of what I called "the finger," of the crucified Christ that hung on my bedroom wall, and of the chain in the collar of my raincoat. "The finger" appeared in a dream when I was about five years old, a dream that consisted solely of a man's index finger emerging from behind a picket fence. My brothers mocked me on the confession of this nightmare by poking their fingers in my face and yelling, "The finger! The finger!" The reaction to the crucified Christ was less an anxiety perhaps than a resistance to or rejection of the ghoulish iconography of Catholicism. I told my mother I couldn't stand to wake to nails piercing Christ's flesh, to blood, to the pain and sadness on his face. So we searched religious gift shops until finding a crucifix with the risen Christ, fully clothed and fully healed, floating on not nailed to its surface. The chain in my raincoat was a double-layered fear. Walking to first grade on a rainy day, I'd hear the little chinking sound the swish of the chain in the collar of my coat would make, and I'd be convinced that it wasn't the chain used to hang my raincoat by but a dog chain, sure sign that a loose dog was in the vicinity, and I was afraid of dogs.

My aversion to man's best friend wasn't helped by the fact that my father's sister, Aunt Bessie, owned ten dogs, who, in what I'm sure was their loving excitement, would, en masse, charge toward me and knock me to the ground whenever we visited. The only ones of my aunt's dogs that I enjoyed were "Tiny," who could fit into the crook of my arm, and "Pepsi," who was perennially old, slow, and who had a great name. Nor was my fear of dogs helped by the fact that a stray pack of mongrels periodically ran along the edge of the yard of our local elementary school. Once, as I walked home from kindergarten, one such creature—a dog twice my size and drooling—planted his paws squarely on my chest and stared into my screaming face. I tripped as I ran from my feisty playmate, a fall that left a hole the size of a quarter in my leotards and in my knee as I watched my milk money roll, beyond reach, into the gutter. But the real source of the fear was maternal inheritance: on walks with my mother, I'd witness her fear of dogs, bequeathed to her by her grandmother, Josephine Conte. Looking through her window onto an Italian countryside, Josephine found a child of hers playing with a rabid dog. Overcome with fear at the sight, she miscarried the child she was pregnant with. From then on, I guess, dogs were to be feared, dogs were to be cursed, and fearing dogs could keep the women on the maternal side of my family close. Fear worn as an amulet.

Reopening the lid on childhood fears makes me wonder if those feelings and perilous scenarios are ever wholly closed off, sealed by the adult mind, apparently spent by youthful revery or conquered by so-called development. Visiting my nephew for the celebration of his tenth birthday recently, I notice that he is looking older, less innocent, more mischievous: he's gaining an edge. And yet even as his child physiognomy appears to be gaining a layer of toughness, I learn that he's developed new fears. His face and fingers smeared with cake and icing after dinner, he taps my brother Anthony's elbow—Uncle Tony, whom he calls "Unc"—and this is all that he says: "Unc," no other words are spoken. It's a secret code that Unc knows means that Joey wants to take his bath now but can't do so alone. My brother explains to me that Joey has had trouble spending time alone in the bathroom since witnessing a scene in *Jurassic Park* in which a man in an outhouse gets eaten by a dinosaur. My nephew lives in cramped quarters—he, his sister, and divorced father sleep in the same bedroom, and the row home is shared with my other brother and father. One would think my nephew—who announced as his New Year's "resolution" one year "to get a bigger house"—would crave rather than fear the privacy of the bathroom. But people rarely seek to understand children's phobias, normal phenomena that, one supposes, will pass in time. Remembering a passage that always stuck with me from *The Notebooks of Malte Laurids Brigge*,

I recall how Rilke knew otherwise: "I am lying in my bed five flights up, and my day, which nothing interrupts, is like a clock-face without hands. As something that has been lost for a long time reappears one morning in its old place, safe and sound, almost newer than when it vanished, just as if someone had been taking care of it—: so, here and there on my blanket, lost feelings out of my childhood lie and are like new. All the lost fears are here again. The fear that a small woolen thread sticking out of the hem of my blanket may be hard, hard and sharp as a steel needle; the fear that this little button on my night-shirt may be bigger than my head, bigger and heavier; the fear that the breadcrumb which just dropped off my bed may turn into glass, and shatter when it hits the floor, and the sickening worry that when it does, everything will be broken, forever; the fear that the ragged edge of a letter which was torn open may be something forbidden, which no one ought to see, something indescribably precious, for which no place in the room is safe enough; the fear that if I fall asleep I might swallow the piece of coal lying in front of the stove; the fear that some number may begin to grow in my brain until there is no more room for it inside me; the fear that I may be lying on granite, on gray granite; the fear that I may start screaming, and people will come running to my door and finally force it open, the fear that I might betray myself and tell everything I dread, and the fear that I might not be able to say anything, because everything is unsayable,—and the other fears . . . the fears. I prayed to rediscover my childhood, and it has come back, and I feel that it is just as difficult as it used to be, and that growing older has served no purpose at all."

Vladimir Nabokov, in *Speak Memory,* reported a similar fear of swelling numbers in his child brain—a fear, I have to say, I never recall having had for myself, but then maybe neither had Nabokov; maybe Nabokov had read Rilke. For Nabokov, unlike Rilke's character, the fear is cured by a mother figure whose "understanding would bring [his] expanding universe back to a Newtonian norm." Could a child really have had the complex, fanciful, subtle and solid, metaphoric and unbounded, symbolic and object-bound, telling, painful, poignant, wise fears that Rilke's adult persona articulates? Or is the point of adulthood to give voice and substance to the vagary of childhood fears, a voice that can never fully be heard, a substance that can never entirely materialize?

After my fall from the high dive, I was lucky, I was even blessed, because there was a kind fellow at the public swim club, a manager who worked for minimum wage, who witnessed the accident, and who found in his heart the desire to take me aside and train me to go back up the ladder of the diving board. He explained to me that if I did not go back off the dive, I'd be haunted by the accident for the rest of my life. He would help me reinvent my relationship to the diving board. I remember how he explained to me that the reason I fell was that I was holding the ladder by its sides and of course if I experienced the slightest imbalance or excitement, that could only lead to a fall, especially if one's hands were tiny and wet. The trick was to grasp the ladder's steps as one climbed. The first time back up, Ray came up with me, standing behind me step by step, then prompting me to plunge into the water and into freedom. The second time, he told me I didn't need him, that surely I could go up alone, and as I emerged from the water, he swung his lifeguard's whistle round his finger, folded his arms, grinned and said: "That's my girl. There's nothing to be afraid of now, is there?" Little did I know that this was the beginning of a working relationship with Ray. He had plans for me: not only was I to master my fear of the dive by going off whenever I chose, but I might consider learning the intricate discipline of diving and become a member of the diving team. Ray taught me how to spring backward off of the lowest board, how to swan dive off the middle board, and how to dive off of the three-meter board, head tucked, hands cuffed to protect my head. I don't remember how exactly I ended our relationship— and thus dashed his plans for a made-for-TV movie—but something in me didn't want to become a competitive diver; something in me did not wish to triumph exactly over my fall from the board. I didn't want to make the fall from the board the basis for my future life, or did I?

Falling from the high dive would prove to take up permanent residence in my psyche as one of many identity themes. I know this because of the way it would return, repeat, transform. Going through the process of gaining tenure as a professor, for example, I developed a fear of falling—a virtually phobic fear of losing motor control as I walked from my office to the campus library. Every step was a trial as I feared (or wished?) that something would give way, and I both craved running into colleagues (to remind me where I was) and feared running into them (lest they would read the terror on my face). Tenure had the unfortunate image of a ladder attached to it, the "tenure ladder," and the unconscious, being not always that clever, even often idiotic, and in my case, in love with the easy metaphor, threw before me once again the threat of the fall from the high dive. It really does seem ridiculous, but it made my living in those days sad and hard. Reading the metaphor, this poem written by a child, and playing it off what I seemed to know to be true, I realized that I wasn't so much afraid of not getting tenure as I was afraid of getting it. For if you weren't in thrall to the past, where would you be? "Nowhere," I would tell myself, and remember the opening lines of a favorite, troubling essay of Emerson's called "Experience": "Where do we find ourselves? In a series of which we do not know the extremes, and believe that it has none. We wake and find ourselves on a stair; there are stairs below us, which we seem to have ascended; there are stairs above us, many a one, which go upward and out of sight. But the Genius which according to the old belief stands at the door by which we enter, and gives us lethe to drink, that we may tell no tales, mixed the cup too strongly, and we cannot shake off the lethargy now at noonday. Sleep lingers all our lifetime about our eyes, as night hovers all day in the boughs of the fir-tree. All things swim and glitter. Our life is not so much threatened as our perception. Ghostlike we glide through nature, and should not know our place again."

As I climbed higher and higher up the ladder of middle class–dom, I surmised, I feared losing my working-class family. Tenure was a pinnacle that would release me, but who wanted to be released? I wanted to be embraced, and through my fears I had been trying to re-embrace my family via my mother, by identifying not with her pleasurable and pleasure-giving self but with the readiest marker of her suffering, of her detachment from me: her phobias, her terror. If I could become my mother, I wouldn't lose her. And if I could become her in her pain, not only would I not forget her, but she would remember me because she would remember that I loved her. Tenure—I could never have anticipated it thus—threatened to cut the connections that defined me. And yet it wasn't as though academia and a life spent reading made up one distinct world while the life of my family or my memory of growing up working class made up another. Treasured walks with my mother to the Darby Library marked the path to academia for me, as did my witnessing of my mother's panic attacks on the Darby Library stairs. Climbing the ladder to the high dive with confidence or trepidation, with Ray behind me or on my own, was already a repetition of mounting that earlier, more significant set of stairs.

I have paused at the threshold of writing these memories—of the trip to the library, of the fall from the dive—for a very long time, convinced, I'm sure, that once I write them, I won't have to make those journeys so suffused with pleasure and pain again; convinced, I'm sure, that once I write them, I will no longer need to repeat them, and afraid therefore of where that would put me, of not knowing then where or who I might be. The Darby Library, distinguished for being the third oldest library in the United States, appeared in *Ripley's Believe It or Not* when in 1947 someone returned a copy of

Richardson's *Clarissa* (an edition from 1764) one hundred years late. I picture the book kept for three generations in a family of literary agoraphobes until someone in the family is finally able to venture out and make the trip back. I, too, keep a book that must be returned to the Darby Library, but it's a book that needs to be written before it can be returned.

CHAPTER 6

The Memory Plant

I didn't know that buttercups were poisonous until I read about them as an adult. According to Pizzetti and Cocker's *Flowers: A Guide for Your Garden*, "all parts of the plant are poisonous, containing an acrid, volatile substance. . . . Ranunculus poisoning, caused by chewing any green part of the plant, is characterized by vomiting, gastric pains, diarrhoea, dizziness, cramps, loss of consciousness, difficulty in breathing, and palpitations. If a stomach pump is not used quickly the victim can die within a day or two." But hadn't I seen cats nuzzle up against and then nibble buttercup leaves? And hadn't the childhood interlude in which you held the flower under your friend's chin, then read the yellow shadow cast there to tell if she liked butter or not, hadn't this required, first or last, the breaking of a buttercup stem between your teeth? Pizzetti and

Cocker tell me, "Apuleius gave the name Horror Plant to the ranunculus because at one time beggars rubbed their legs with the foliage, thereby creating horrible sores and blisters to arouse compassion." By this account, my reckless handling at six years old of the buttercup plant that I dug up from a nearby lot, or, better, tugged up, fist over fist, to transplant to my father's garden, should have led to a monstrous bubbling up of sores. At the end of this story, I would sit mutely before my buttercups, my hands wrapped in white gauze, sorry that I ever disturbed the flowers. I would have learned some kind of lesson. A movie would be made about my tragedy.

I don't know what compelled me at age six to transplant a bunch of buttercups from the local non-playground at the bottom of our street to my father's garden. I don't know if my buttercups were of the cursed, bristly, early, hispid, creeping, bulbous, or common variety. They were yellow. They were possibly the only living thing to be found at "the Lot." "The Lot" so-called—and why not, it *was* an abandoned lot—was the nearest neighborhood open space to play in. In summer, if we played there, we'd have to expect to step on a rusty nail or jagged piece of glass. In winter, we'd hopefully know to steer our sleds in such a way so as not to end up in the middle of the highway the slope of the Lot abutted. In autumn, we swung Tarzan-style from a rope attached to the Lot's one tree—until my best friend swung smack into a rusted shopping cart at the Lot that scarred her face forever. Maybe I dug up those buttercups because I knew the Lot was no place for living things. Maybe I wanted to show that I, too, could be a gardener, or that

I wanted something that was my own in the garden, or that I wanted my father's companionship. Maybe, like my father, I wanted to make things grow.

The only detail I recall about digging up the buttercups is that it was laborious—their roots ran deep to my child hands. And I remember running, not coolly walking, home with them to present to my father, to explain to him that I intended to plant them in the yard. When I'd left for my buttercup excursion, my father had been kneeling over a bed of fancy petunias in the front yard, loud singing trumpeters that reminded me of the matted velour collar of a favorite sweater. Now he was no longer there. But something told me not to look for him in the house—certainly not to track the loosening soil from my now drooping plant into the house—but to run around the block to the backyard, where he would probably be found kneeling to inspect the new shoots of his lunaria or pruning his roses. I could see that the garden gate was open as I ran up the driveway. I could see the line of the gardening hose crossing like a snake from the garage up the garden steps. And the silver watering can glinting from the base of the slope where it sat. The buttercups were losing more dirt as I ran, and a few of the stems that had held the yellow cups were now draped like strands of spaghetti over my hands, their blooms closed and wilted. I needed my father to resuscitate them, and then to help me find a place for them in our home.

Running into the garden, I was almost stopped short by my father's familiar, unperturbable garden posture: crouched into a position that transmuted his body into a perfectly shaped letter "C," he was no longer himself but a form of benediction. When he assumed this position, only my mother could rouse him by shouting: "What! Are you going to take root out there?!" I was only *almost* stopped short, for, knowing better than to speak, I still thrust my glorious handful of dirt and roots and flecks of yellow petals into his line of vision. He held his hand, palm facing forward, up to his face as though he were shielding himself from an invading light. Then he turned to me and spoke in gentle—his morning prayers had mellowed him—though mocking tones. "What are you doing, Mary? Where did you get those? Are you trying to help me weed the garden?" My father's breath was often somewhat sour, but as he said this, his mouth looked sweet.

"These are buttercups," I said. "The buttercups I found at the Lot so we could plant them."

"You don't plant buttercups," my father said. "Buttercups are weeds."

I didn't respond. He repeated the sentence, this time pronouncing each word more loudly, more boldly, and leaving too much space between them: "Buttercups. Are. Weeds. Now throw them on the compost pile."

Exhaling, I pretended not to hear him: "These buttercups will stop breathing if we do not plant them."

Waiting for my father's response, I heard the sound of his small spade hit the soil. I heard his heels dig into the earth as he pulled himself into an upright position. "Bring your buttercups around to the front of the house," he said.

I made the journey back down the driveway, only stopping

temporarily to balance the buttercups in one hand while closing with the other the garden gate. Back around the bottom of the drive and up Concord Road's steep hill. I made the backward journey slowly as though the encounter to win my father over to my cause had exhausted me, and I watched my drooping bunch bounce in slow motion with each tired step. I fancied the yellow blossoms a satin accompaniment to the petunia's velour, a sweetener to the sour marigolds, new small friends to the high-rising roses, at the same time that I expected defeat.

Having arrived again at the front door, I placed the plant at the bottom of the steps where I sat looking down on it as though the plant would die if I failed to watch it. Sitting on the front steps of the house waiting for my father, I marked time by the sporadic visits to the half-open buttercups by what must have been starving bees. After a while, my father came through the front door of the house carrying the small spade. He told me I could dig a hole for the buttercups in the cramped and heavily shaded triangle of earth at the base of the hedge— the shallow patch of dirt that met the cement in front of the house, hardly part of the garden at all.

If buttercups like an open, airy position in full sun, why, then, did my father consign them to the darkest part of our garden? Of course he knew that buttercups are weeds and he didn't want them to overtake the yard. That they grew at all, out of their element, is a wonder. Each year I marked my father's surprise and even joy at their return. "*Ranunculus ficaria* are one of the first signs of Spring, even before the sun's rays have any real warmth and before the cuckoo begins to call" (Pizzetti and Cocker). Every year the buttercups beneath the hedge came back. They come back. Every year they come back to my father's house even though I'm not there to see them.

Certainly a gardener could not have buttercups overrunning the yard, especially if he wished to grow lunaria, which demanded a certain space and protection. The cultivation of lunaria was one of my father's most interesting gardening experiments. Pizzetti and Cocker have written that the lunaria is also commonly referred to as "honesty," "satin flower," "moon wort," "silver shilling," or "St. Peter's pence." To us, it was known as the "silver dollar" or "money plant." The names make sense since, once dried (and the whole point of growing lunaria is to dry them), lunaria turns into a pale yellow or chalk white stalk that sports a series of thinner-than-paper silvery disc-shaped membranes reminiscent of full moons, or of a clear view (honesty), or of coins.

My father sowed each flat and round seed, each imprinted with what looks like the footprint of a tiny bird, then waited two years to gather, prepare, disseminate, and attempt to market his small crop. Lunaria's first year went practically unnoticed in the garden—it could easily be mistaken for an ungainly weed with unctuous flowers. In its second year, the plant became thoroughly lime green as it developed and yielded its circular seedpods. My father would harvest the plants now and hang them, batlike, upside down in the garage. When they were sufficiently dried and drained of their color, he would call on me (I was ten or eleven years old) to help him painstakingly remove each seedpod's outer casement to reveal the singular silver disc beneath.

Maybe because I was the child of industry—always doggedly involved in my schoolwork, Saturday's child, born to work for a living—my father thought I would want to spend the better part of a prepubescent Saturday afternoon bent over the money plants with him in the garage. The smell of motor oil mingled there with the smells of summer: overripe garbage and the lavender my father had planted near the garage. In our miniature sweatshop, why hadn't we been manufacturing perfume? My father would prepare makeshift stools for each of us out of the Charles Chips cookie drums that he used for storing rock salt, then proceed with the ground rules for removing the seed casings. While anyone's first impulse might be to peel off the disc's outer shell, my father showed me that the better approach was to rub the parchment-colored casing gently between thumb and forefinger until both sides of the sandwiched moon fell away to expose the light within. At the same time, the pod's brown seeds would fall to the floor or stick to your wrist or cling to the moonish membrane. The seedpods had a waxen feel, and sometimes, to get a better purchase on them, I grasped them too aggressively, crumpling their inner moons in the process. Thus our little meeting was not without a few "God-damn-its," a few "Give-me-thats," yelled out by my father, a few phrases, too, whose words I've forgotten but that translated as jolts at the base of my throat and stomach.

In its better mood, the process of preparing the money plant reminded me of the time I lost a fingernail, but without the terror that accompanied that falling away, without the fear that came at the moment of losing each first tooth. Preparing the decorative stems of the money plant reminded me a little of the hours spent in an earlier year applying with a small brush my choice of paint and sparkles to pine cones laid out on a place mat made of newspaper at the kitchen table, later to hang the now pseudo-pine cones on the pseudo-tree we mounted at Christmas. A space opened in the usually crowded and noisy kitchen; a silence settled there. But where painting pine cones meant the addition of a coat of color to the tree's seedpods, the preparation of the money plant called for subtraction. The first time I saw the shed skin of a garter snake (only in adulthood), I recognized lunaria's kin: the same slip of shimmering film, the same deceptively thin density. To prepare lunaria was to aid in a process of molting.

Thinking back on lunaria, I daydream that their discs must yield a music if touched upon by the wind—a high-pitched single note available only to a particular species of bird or insect or furry creature: hummingbird or dragonfly or fox. But this would be to translate them into heavenly spheres or to lay them on the compost heap of bad Romantic poetry when, really, lunaria, in my family's world at least, took two very distinct and practical routes.

My father gave a number of lunaria away to interested neighbors and to each of his Sicilian family members. What remained, he attempted to sell. While my mother's Neapolitan family, I'm sure, also filled a vase or two with the fruit of my father's lunaria, I do not remember lunaria sharing the same pride of place there that they did in the households of my father's extended family. Each Sicilian interior might have borne the singular stylistic mark of its owner, but that distinction was ultimately no more than a blurred backdrop for the three items that every household contained and displayed like familial fetishes: a brightly colored wooden model of a horse-drawn cart; a huge and gaudy plaster bust of Giuseppe Verdi; a vase of my father's silver dollars.

My grandmother, Ninfa, used to let me play with the colorful cart when I was a child, though I remember its being a frustrating toy: the figurines who peopled the cart were made of cast iron, so they were confined to one position, their hands painted onto their laps, their heads immovable. I did discover, however, that they could be removed from their seat in the cart, but the revelation led to some discomfort. Each figure had a hole drilled into its bottom that enabled it to fit loosely onto a spike coming up through the cart's bench. Once I'd removed the figurines, I had a hard time putting them back without imagining pain. To this day, no one has quite explained to me the meaning of what I think was called "the Contadina cart." What I saw when I looked at it were royally regaled horses drawing a cart filled with peasants. Was the cart a kind of national coat of arms or Sicilian banner? I might have to read a book to know.

Alongside the cart, as I have said, each family planted an armless white bust of Verdi. I don't know what inspired my father's father to purchase the busts, one for each of his four children sometime in the 1970s. A hierarchy inhered between my mother's and father's sides of the family that led me to believe that the Sicilians, unlike the Neapolitans and Compobassans, had no interest in or love of opera. The combination of my mother's possessiveness and my father's detachment from his family engendered a class bias toward my Sicilian relatives that led me naively, stupidly, to figure them in my mind as less cultured. Now I know that each side of the family had its own "culture," its own modes of literacy, its own cuisine, its own brand of storytelling, its own survival strategies, its own ethic, its own equal share of kitsch and high art—and where does one draw the line between them? But I had learned to be more observant and respectful of one over the other, and this spoke of the riven-ness of my parents' union as much as it did an immigrant or white ethnic ethos in America that, in the name of class differentiation, would pit Italians against each other and against people of color, whom they, after all, resembled.

The only time I'd ever been to an opera was with my Sicilian, not my Neapolitan, grandfather. I was thirteen years old and the opera was *Aida*. Unfortunately, the cheap seats afforded us a wholly vertiginous view, and I remember, between dizziness and nausea, wondering if those life-sized horses were the same ones that pulled the carts back home. These are the things my Sicilian grandfather wanted to purchase with his retirement money from his job as sheet metal worker at the Philadelphia Naval Base: opera tickets, busts of Verdi, and an annual extended family feast in the banquet room of a nearby restaurant.

I remember my mother wincing when my father's siblings referred to the bust of Verdi as "Joe Green." One brother-in-law even painted the quill pen that lay beneath Verdi's chin a shade of cheap canary. As for our bust, it remained chalky white and so finely chiseled that I remember having to wipe dust out of Verdi's nostrils. My father, for various reasons, clearly didn't share his family's buoyancy or tendencies toward fun. I could tell, although I could not tell why, that they really did not want him, and I even secretly wished on occasion that my father's more beloved brother, Sammy, was my dad. My Uncle Sammy occasionally got into some mild trouble that my father was expected to bail him out of. In my father's single years, he'd send his paycheck from his job in the armed services to his mother for safekeeping. But when he returned home from his duty, his mother told him the money was gone—she'd given it to Sammy to pay for his divorce. Consequently, my father's smile never matched my Uncle Sammy's wide and glorious grin.

My Uncle Sammy also cooked—spicy sauces and sausage, ravioli he cut by hand, and bread he kneaded. My father could not eat his family's food—all of it uniformly made him sick. At how many multicourse Sicilian family feasts had I watched the shrunken figure of my father nurse a cup of tea with lemon? There was a period of years when my father seemed to survive on Pepperidge Farm frozen layer cake—it was the only food I ever saw him attack with gusto. He'd qualify most other indulgences even in the midst of them with the sad phrase: "I'll pay for this tomorrow." Food bound my father's family to each other, confirmed their attachments, spoke for and through them. My father sat on the outskirts of these conversations, starving and occasionally yelling. My father's siblings and parents, cousins, uncles and aunts, were close to each other but not to him, and so I could not get inside them either. A tiny piece of the puzzle was his choice to leave the city (and South Philly in particular) for the suburbs when he married, rather late at twenty-eight, to refuse the part they may have had in store for him: to remain single and care for his parents. My father was outside the forms of his family's desiring. Maybe this is why he grew that kitschy "money" plant in his garden to give to them—because he wanted a way to be of them and with them and recognized by them.

I never finished out the ritual of preparing lunaria with my father. There was stacking and bundling to be done after the stripping of the seedpods. But I'd brush myself off at a point, too hurt by his eternally sour face, then ask my father, "Can I go now?" He would tell me to go; he would finish up alone. Consulting a Sicilian friend about the Contadina cart, I learn of more misreadings on my part. The animals that drive the cart are not horses but donkeys. The donkey in Sicilian culture has a status similar to the pig in other cultures—it is an ambivalent mixture of high and low, near and far, respect and abjection. The knowledge jars my memory: how vividly I recall my brother wincing as my father kicked him in the ass—and what could a small boy have done to deserve such harm?—and the name that he called him as he kicked him: not horse's ass, but "donkey." My father— neither is he above or below contradiction. He is the man who uses his hands—those same that tend the most beautifully delicate garden in the neighborhood—to beat his two sons. Until the day my mother, upheaving a large knife out from within a chaos of utensils crashing onto the kitchen floor, threatens to kill my father if he dares to touch my brothers ever again.

If carefully handled they will last for years . . .

PIZZETTI AND COCKER,

FLOWERS: A GUIDE FOR YOUR GARDEN

Lunaria held these practical places in my family: they were the gift that my father gave to his city-dwelling relatives from his suburban garden; they were the pretext for time spent between him and me. But lunaria do not stop at these doors. They tempt me, like a drunk to his drug, to metaphor.

Because it takes two seasons, two years to become itself, lunaria isn't what it seems at first. It has more than one incarnation. Rather than call it the money plant, I would therefore insist that it be known as the memory plant. If *never* handled, memories will persist for years.

According to Pizzetti and Cocker, "Lunarias reached their maximum popularity in the nineteenth century, when all types of dried flowers, leaves, seeds, and even wax fruits, were so popular in the Victorian drawing-room. Occasionally, and with the greatest patience, these small moon-like seed-bearing cases were hand-painted with designs." The Victorians painted scenes onto the discs? This to me is like purposely clouding a clarity or pulling a shade down on a window. The lunaria doesn't want to be applied to but looked through.

It's not what it seems.

It doesn't let me fasten on it.

Each disc on a stem clicks open like a camera's shutter or the clicking into place of multiple lenses before the optometrist's screen. What can I read there? What make out? In a second incarnation, lunaria discs burst like a camera's flash leaving spots before my eyes and foggy after-images in their beyond.

What is lunaria most like? What past forms share its shape or its surface, its depth and delicacy, its tenuous poise? In one flash, the Host; in another, a glass eye. Closing my eyes to open them again, now lunaria is an uncrossable patch of ice; now a pane of glass I wish to break through. I must stop this, or I'll become metaphor-crazed, the world reduced to spots before my eyes begging for translation. Are all these images, memory's scenes, too much for the lunaria to carry?

The Host. Paper-thin monument to Christ's body. You weren't allowed to chew it, but sometimes I noticed people doing so. I did not like the thought the priest put into my head when he pressed the tablike wafer onto my tongue—"Body of Christ"—the thought of eating flesh. Of course, I ruined my first Holy Communion ceremony, so how could I expect ever to enjoy the Host properly? At eight years old, I had learned to pronounce and spell the words "sacristy," "tabernacle," "consecrate," but I hadn't honored my teachers by showing that I'd understood their meaning by venerating the Host, the visiting bishop, or his miter. I was, though, dressed in white from top to toe, and my mother had allowed a neighborhood hairdresser to remove my curls and leave me with a short, straight nunlike pixie for the ceremony. Renounce all but the whiteness of whiteness. The purity of Christ's body. Priests got to drink his blood. I talked and laughed with another little girl through my entire first communion ceremony. It was as though the incense were laughing gas. We giggled and giggled, tickling each other, then pretending innocence. We could barely contain our hilarious hope that the bishop's tall hat, shaped like somebody's backside, would topple from his bald head. I felt only vaguely guilty about having had so much fun with another little girl during the solemn ritual that would give us the benefit of recognizing and confessing our eight-year-old sins. Until I arrived home and discovered that I'd somehow brought home another girl's purse. The purse, I could now see, was nothing like mine—it obviously belonged to a slob. All it contained was a cheap and tattered Bible and a dirty plastic statue of a naked baby Jesus. I rifled through its empty chamber feeling as though something terrible had happened. The last time I had had this feeling was in kindergarten when I awoke from naptime to find that the picture of the squirrel I had colored for my mother—my first success at staying within the lines—was no longer in the cubby hole where I had left it. Somebody stole it, I thought, as I walked home empty-handed and in tears. Someone would give it to *her* mother, but what would I give to mine? Where was my purse? In what daze had I left it behind? How could I possibly have confused this one with my own? Had the stupid, dirty little girl who owned this purse carried mine home? Mine was a mini–treasure chest with my gloves folded neatly to form a pillow for my rosaries. I'd placed a scapular in there, some holy cards, a favorite pencil and its sharpener, dried daisy petals from the previous year's May Day celebration, and my Bible with its splendid white leather cover and gold-embossed cross. It was the Bible that had been my mother's as a girl. There was such a void in this other little girl's purse that you could hear the plastic baby Jesus bouncing around inside. My purse didn't make a sound, and I was proud of that. God was punishing me, I thought, by replacing my treasures with emptiness, by taking my favorite Bible away and showing me what I really deserved and what was really important: an ugly Bible and the (naked) body of Christ. If this was the lousy gift God gave me for my first communion, to whom did he give my purse? Probably to the little girl who had nothing and was happy nonetheless. To the little girl who sat quietly during her first communion. But she wouldn't know what to make of my things, I kept insisting to myself. She wouldn't appreciate them the way I did.

The next time I was given a Bible, it was a gift from the first woman I'd ever fallen in love with as an adult. At the time I met Julia, she was busy denying and repenting her lesbianism by desperately trying to be "born again," so the closest our relationship came to consummation was the evening she whispered the entire sultry text of the Song of Solomon into my ear in the college library. That night in my dorm room, I wrote a passionate poem to Julia that I read aloud to my friends. When asked whom the poem was for, I told my friends, "Jesus Christ." They freaked out more than if I'd said "Julia." They thought I might be one step away from joining a cult. The Bible Julia gave me had a maroon leather cover which opened to her inscription penned on its white inside leaf:

7 July 1980. Dear Mary, I give this Bible to you with the deepest love of friendship in Christ, in His perfect Love, that the literature and poetry of

*these pages would reveal the person of Jesus Christ, the reality of redemp-
tion, the fullness of His Life. To two hearts jostling in one yellow ray of summer—I love you Mary, Julia.*

A few years prior to this, I had found another replacement
for my lost Bible in a volume of *Anna Karenina* I tried to read.
It was maybe the first book I took seriously into my hands and
into my solitude in early adolescence. It, too, had a white cover
and it was about the same size and length as the lost Bible. I
read from it as though I were praying, but really I was worship-
ing at the altar of Art, and barely able to contain how Tolstoy's
and Anna's passion roused me.

A glass eye. Once on a trip to see my mother's sister Frances,
who lived nearby, and her daughter, my cousin Rosemarie, my
brothers and I were told that other cousins from Rosemarie's
father's side of the family would be there too, including a
woman with a glass eye. I was about nine years old, and the unknown cousin was about seventeen. I don't remember much
about this visit except that I latched onto this woman's defect.
I noticed that only one of her eyes moved, but that both of her
eyes were beautiful, blue, and she had luscious blonde hair. She
had a confident, all-American co-ed quality about her and yet
it seemed as if the whole side of her body that held the glass eye
was stiff. I imagined that she was in pain, but I don't think I was
afraid of her so much as I was afraid of what she represented—
that all of the crazy fears my father chanted to us daily might
have a basis in reality.

About any toy smaller than a hand: "You'd better be careful or you might swallow that."

About jump ropes: "You'd better look out or you might trip on the darn thing and break your ankle."

Before going to bed: Lock all doors *and* windows; close all shades, blinds, and curtains; turn off all lights; unplug all appliances (except the refrigerator and alarm clock).

Never take a bath or shower during a rainstorm: lightning could strike you through the skylight.

Going for a drive: fasten all seat belts and keep doors locked at all times. "Put your belt on," my father would say, or "Do you have your belt on?" He never called it a *seat* belt, and whenever he said "fasten your belt," I'd feel the sick feeling I associated with *his* belt. Did he have *his* belt on? Or was he going to take it off and thrash us with it as he sometimes did?

About almost any new toy, no matter its shape, size, or premise: "That could knock your eye out" / "Be careful or you'll knock somebody's eye out." My father led us to think of the world as a place where unidentified projectiles could at any time take you unawares and change your life forever. I had never seen anyone's eye fall out, but my father used this rhetoric so often—"You could knock somebody's eye out with that"—that it made me wonder if human physiology operated on the same principle as my Mr. Potatohead dolls.

My blonde cousin was living proof that someone could knock someone else's eye out. In fact, my parents explained to me, she'd lost her eye to a model plane made of balsa wood that her brother accidentally steered in her direction. I already knew the story of how Sally Starr (another blonde beauty) lost an eye—they'd tell me about that whenever I pulled my winter coat off its hanger by its sleeve rather than by its collar. Hangers could knock an eye out.

And then of course there was the extent to which malevolent eyes figured in the folklore of my father's culture—was this one of the origins of his fears? The idea that *malocchio*, the evil eye, could strike you anytime, that someone could *give* you the evil eye, as my relatives said, and in that giving, a curse, bad luck, suffering, an unfortunate end. I understood then why one of Sicily's patron saints was Lucy—the saint who had her eyes knocked out. (In the picture books, she carried them on a plate). And the jewelry that some Sicilian Americans might wear to ward off the evil eye featured the notion that, if need be, one could pierce the evil eye. Citing folkloric origins for my father's fears doesn't really help me to understand his preoccupation with blindness.

I only know that I didn't want my father's fears to be ratified by my unknown cousin's glass eye, for if I agreed to live in the same world as the one painted by his fears, there would be no corner from which pleasure might wave and say, "Hello." I tried to picture my Guardian Angel with this cousin's face. I tried to picture her smiling at me as if to say that even though some part of her was gone from her, a life-giving revelation had taken its place, leaving her without fear. The fantasy would barely last a second before her face would turn sad, somewhere between tears and tearlessness.

An uncrossable patch of ice. I'm sitting in the back seat of our 1965 Ford Falcon, occupying the middle seat, or "hump" as we called it, since my elder brothers have, as usual, won the side windows. We've just arrived home from a visit to my mother's parents' house. It's the middle of winter. My brothers have jumped out of the car and are already racing to the back door. I haven't left the car because my eight-year-old eyes have caught the glimpse of terror on my mother's face. My father has already headed out, so this just leaves Mom and me to face the fact that she cannot get out of the car. Getting out would mean crossing a small patch of ice, and my mother becomes immobilized with fear in the face of ice. You could say that faced with ice, my mother becomes it—frozen as the thing itself—while it, the ice, becomes something other than itself, my mother's private metaphor. It scares me when my mother gets like this, when she becomes that lady I don't recognize because this particular lady would not recognize me—I know I do not exist in this lady's purview, whereas to my mother, I am the world. All she sees is what she's seeing that I can't see, and I'm not in the picture. I don't remember if my mother tells me to get my father because this is a job for fearless Joe (ha, ha), but I do remember that I beckon to my father from the car rather than run from the car to get him. Either I believe my mother and I are equally stranded in the car by the uncrossable glacier that has surrounded us in the minute that the men left the vehicle or I don't want to leave her alone—they're both the same really—because I've bent myself over the front seat and have rolled down the driver's side window to call to my father to help us: "Dad. Dad. Help! Help! Mommy can't get out of the car!"

My parents' fears are of a different depth and order from each other, which maybe means there's hope that they can help each other. This wasn't the first time I'd witnessed my mother's paralysis before a patch of ice, but I don't recall outside of this incident my father becoming so theatrical, so playful in the face of her fear that I could almost love him. Exasperated by the reasoned talk meant to tempt her out of the car and into his arms, he gives in to an impulse to dance. He says, "Look, Rosemary, look here, look at me," as he jumps, twirls, and lets his feet move out from under him every which way without his falling. I laugh and feel so thankful to my father for making me laugh and for letting my mother know in this way that he loves her, that the world is not wholly a dangerous place. He *did* have a clownish side; he *could* have fun.

He laid out his gig as though he were putting down his coat as a carpet for her to step on. Then I remember my mother agreeing to let my father pull her from the car and her sound—"Oh"—as he carried her across the ice, "Oh," like the sound a person makes when the doctor has to reset a bone by hand or replace a dislocation, just that kind of quick consensual movement. As my parents hobbled into the house, I shut and locked the car doors and skipped inside behind them. I thought my mother would be happy that my father rescued her, but she wasn't. She was rarely happy after these episodes even though from my point of view she'd won; she was home; she'd made it to the other side. As for me, I might have been skipping, but something froze in me that day that would replay for more years than I could count like an uncomplicated music box ditty: the words of the song were muted, but the tune and rhythm sent the message to me in little pulses—that I must always be aware, and especially when I might be having fun, especially if I were laughing, that my mother could be in pain.

Now I look back on the episode and I find myself wondering if the person phobically caught on one side of a patch of ice fears the substance for its opacity or its transparency? Is the fear of ice bound up with a fear of what one cannot see? The ground, if opacity. The ice itself, if transparency. Probably that wasn't the basis of my mother's fear; probably it had something to do with mine.

A pane of glass I wish to break through. Lunaria reminds me of the Host and of a glass eye and of an unpassable patch of ice. But it also reminds me of an image that would come to me periodically—for lack of a better way to put it—of moving through a window without causing breakage or harm. Fantasies of permeability. Lately, I've had the feeling, I don't know how else to put it, that my perception of the world has been "spotty." It's not the kind of feeling I readily share with people. Maybe if I had stayed with the sciences longer, I'd have a way of describing this that wouldn't sound crazy. When I have this feeling, I can moor it in poetic abstraction by asking, for example, whether a spot of time (as in a spotty sense of time or space) is equivalent to the frantic puff of one's breath into a party favor or more like the gentle though reluctant puffs with which I blow on the figure that I imagine of a thimble-sized princess who appears before my face and beckons me to kiss her—the kiss is not allowed. When I have this feeling, I can moor it in quasi-scientific abstraction as well: if time happens in spots rather than lines, it occurs to me, permeability seems immanent.

Highly privatized imagery like this, I realize, might not help me to clarify or communicate my state of mind, which is to say, my state of memory. It may only have the effect of helping me to foster the illusion that what is strange in me is at least my own. Do I share with the Victorians the desire to make lunaria "keepsakes," or am I the more precious one? Have I misunderstood their project entirely? Painting on the surface of lunaria, the Victorians were not, as I have pictured them, blocking lunaria's view. They were exploiting the place between opacity and transparency, lunaria's translucence. Such depictions marked onto lunaria's helpful surface could only be viewed when held up to a light or by backlighting the lunaria. Lunaria gets us out of at the same time as it complicates the either/or bind of total blockage or total recall of the past.

In fact I'd like to believe that lunaria's translucence is what has enabled it to bear all my metaphors: much can be borne on a surface that blocks some light while letting other light through. Writing on lunaria's surface, I want to feel like Neil Armstrong bouncing, not walking, on the moon. Unlike the Victorians', though, I hope my magic lantern slides are not appropriate for the drawing room.

Talking to my father recently about his own occasional

jottings, wondering what, if any light from the past passes through the screen of his present, I discovered a stunning resemblance between an image he recorded in a piece he wrote for himself called "Childhood Memories" and the association I had conjured between our lunaria and a pane of glass. My father is pleased that he can remember details of his childhood because he believes his ability to remember is a sign that his parents loved him. The parcel of memories he records is compact: in one memory, his mother is bathing him; in the next, his parents are taking him, at age three, to a relative's wake. My father explains that he'd been sleeping, but awoke to see his parents dressed up to go out. His crying led them to take him with them, but he couldn't know that the outing was a mournful affair, and he was forever after haunted by the sight of the dead body. The next memory has him falling backward from the chair whose back rungs he is perched on. The person seated in the chair hadn't known that he was balanced there, and when the adult rose from the chair, my father fell back, hitting his head on a radiator. The main detail of this memory is that though the blow was severe enough to warrant stitches, my father did not cry. An ice cream cone was his reward. The final memory he records is of a dream:

I remember my very first dream or more rightly, I should say, the first dream I can remember. I was two or three years old. Well anyhow it was sometime before my fourth birthday and it goes like this. The dream that is. I was looking out of the front door to see what I could see through a full pane of clear glass. There was absolutely nothing going on out there. Hon-

estly! Now here comes the best part. Then I put my hand up to my forehead
and right in the center of it I felt a hole about the size of a quarter. Don't
laugh! Being curious, as all children are, I poked my finger into it. It felt
like it was filled with straw. Please! Don't laugh! Remember, I was still
just a baby. I suppose by this time you're thinking that the straw is still
there.

Is it only I who associate straw with donkeys, or is that association commonplace enough to warrant the interpretation that
from a very young age my father was taught to think of himself
as an ass? Had my father overheard someone tell someone else
that the person had a hole in his head? Or had someone said
that to him? What fear or desire is implicit in a dream of a
viewless vista? And what of my pane of glass, what of my experience of the holes in time's netting? Were these my father's
images, my father's memories, or my own? What's the significance of a familial iconography marked by encounters
with nothingness?

Maybe none of us has "our own" memory, but each of us
inherits the memories of our ancestors, while what distin-
guishes us is our interpretation of those pasts. My father internalized the void, and convinced himself he was as good
as nothing. When emptiness threatens me, my weapon is to
read it.

My family has me so well trained to read metaphorically,
or I learned through them to read metaphorically to survive,
that I am not really sure it's possible for me to look at anything
directly. But I am trying to learn how to follow my meta-

phors—so many spots before my eyes—which is not to say give in to them or give over to them but only not to fight them or to too painfully grope.

Memory of course does not always or only take the form of narrative. That's something we have to force it to do. Often enough it takes the form of a texture or shape, a symbol or metaphor. The aura of my grandfather's shoe repair shop and writing studio, for example, comes back to me, in part, in the form of a plant—a particularly scary and abundantly healthy cactus called euphorbia. Having heard the plant referred to as "the crown of thorns," my cousin Rosemarie and I would dare each other as children to break a stem of the heavily spiked plant to prove the milky substance we were told it contained really did exist: unto us, Christ's blood. But neither of us ever had the guts to do it. If I want to get the plant to speak—and in that way enable me to say something *I* need to say while at the same time keeping me from facing something directly—I turn to metaphor. I notice a connection between the euphorbia and lunaria, and thus between the Sicilian and Neapolitan influences in my life: both plants can be said to yield the perfume of religious dogma—lunaria is a member of the Cruciferae family, meaning crosslike or bearing a cross, and euphorbia, we will recall, invokes a crucifixion. Euphorbia, for me, is a much harder text than lunaria to read. It's not so much a story as a symbol, and a symbol of Italian American immigrant suffering at that—a symbol of suffering whose code I feel I need to crack, the cross described in my immigrant grandfather's journals. He writes: "Pirandello was right in saying: and I quote, 'In life every man wears a mask.' The mask, however, is like the cross: no matter how light it may be, its weight in the end is unbearable." Even in his more hopeful sentences, this cross still accompanies him: "What I loved, love and shall love is not within my reach, but it has helped to bear my cross." I had learned to love to read.

CHAPTER 7

The Body Will Tell

There were things about my mother that I knew without her ever having told me. There were things that she carried that she may not have wanted to burden me with but that she invited me to read nevertheless. This unspoken legacy operated in the formation of my own subjectivity even if I couldn't name its details and qualities directly. The most *unsayable*, the most indiscernible, and yet most pervasively present of these were my mother's active contemplation of suicide in the years that she suffered most from agoraphobia, in her thirties, and the poor material conditions—the poverty—of her earliest years.

I don't remember being conscious of the fact that my mother considered suicide as a way out of the desperation that often overcame her. But a turning point in her own attitude toward survival led to a revelation in me. I was a senior in college, and I had spoken to my mother on the telephone every

Sunday of the fours years of my undergraduate career. One day my mother called me with special news. She had an announcement to make, something important that she wanted me to know, she said.

She said that she'd had a breakthrough in her psychotherapy, and that it led to a momentous decision. She explained how for years she'd kept a bottle of pills on her desk that she would consider overdosing herself with, but that today she had washed the pills down the drain. She'd chosen life now, and the pills could no longer maintain their symbolic power. The therapist she had been seeing had been recommended to her the last time she'd called the Suicide Control Center. She had made an appointment, then canceled it, but when he called back to ask if that was a pattern of hers—to seek help and then not follow through on getting it—she rescheduled the appointment. It was one of the best decisions she had ever made.

I don't know how I took this news in. The announcement of my mother's decision to live made wholly visible her one-time desire to die, and it was hard to tell if her ongoing dialogue with self-destruction was new knowledge to me or old. Did I retreat to my dorm room and weep? Did I continue blithely through the day, meet friends for pizza, play pinball, study for exams? Did I call my friends together to tell them about the wild conversation I'd had with my mother? I suspect I went to the library to continue working on my term paper for my class "Psychology and Shakespeare." It was entitled "Ophelia and Lady Macbeth: A Psychoanalytic View of Suicide and Womanhood." The subject had been a perfectly respectable and therefore perfectly detached topic of intellectual

inquiry before I spoke to my mother. "Freud never totally rec-
onciled suicide with his psychoanalytic paradigm," the student writes on page 1, "thus making the student's inquiry into
the ultimate self-destructive act all the more exciting, if frustrating." On page 2, she states her thesis: "While Lady Macbeth and Ophelia are almost antithetical character-types,
while their separate modes of leave-taking are suited to their
unique conflicts, they share the inability to assert a 'true self,'
to achieve personal fulfillment in an altruistically oriented and
male-dominated world. This leads one to explore not only the
motivations of Ophelia and Lady Macbeth, but the societal
and psychic elements which enable Hamlet and Macbeth to
survive in a real world without committing suicide." That day,
I sat in my study carrel reading and rereading my paper. It was
both disarming and oddly comforting to realize that my paper,
whose material had seemed so new to me, was motivated by
something about which I already knew a great deal but had
not acknowledged. Certain of the paper's details now lit up:
"Moreover, the closeness between the members of Ophelia's
family—Laertes, Polonius and herself—the fact that they become concerned with each other's lives to the point of inter-
ference, the fact that they interact within the confines, what
Hamlet calls the prison, of the state of Denmark, further in-
hibits Ophelia's ego-development. Laertes, at least, has the opportunity to travel to France; Hamlet, at least, is permitted to
study abroad. As Freud writes, 'The more closely the members
of a family are attached to one another, the more often do they
tend to cut themselves off from others, and the more difficult is
it for them to enter into the wider circle of life.' . . . 'Ophelia'

means help—implying her dependence in living and her consequent cry for help in suicide."

Looking back on the paper from a distance of nearly twenty years, I dwell over the professor's comments as though I'm the girl who wrote the paper again, a girl who, though receptive, does not take criticism well. The paper earns an "A," and yet it has "weaknesses"—the professor has listed them next to the paper's "strengths." The qualities he's penned at the top of the list are most interesting to me now: "Strength: plethora of suggestive verbal connections." "Weakness: verbal ties, some rather fanciful, are too dominant. They should come *after* more obvious evidence." It's confusing. The strength and the weakness of my analysis are one and the same. As such, they speak to my greatest talent and my most ready defense mechanism—the ability to make words work and the tendency to disappear into words. What the professor had highlighted was the opportunity I had taken all my life to use language—that most flimsy, unpredictable, unreliable of substances—to hold something close. Linguistic subtlety and nuance were considered a strength. Linguistic hyperbole was a weakness. If the ability to find similarity in seemingly disparate things defined the power of artists as metaphor makers, the compulsion to make metaphor was a symptom, a sickness one might consider treating. Hasty leaps are cop-outs: the sublime must be earned, not leapt into.

I recognize to this day how easily subtlety loops into hyperbole, how readily nuance becomes overdetermination in my work, and I read that tic as my compensation for the anxiety provoked by the indeterminate space between absence and presence in which all selfhood resides. I think, though, that children of parents who threaten to disappear on a daily basis experience that normally discomforting space even more precariously and acutely than others. When my mother was present, she was overwhelmingly present; when my mother was absent, she was devastatingly absent. The offspring of such conditions are people who interpret and desire reality as an all-or-nothing option.

My college paper on Shakespeare's Ophelia and Lady Macbeth was neither the first nor the last time that the silent specter of fear of loss of my mother would try to speak in an academic context. Last year, for instance, at a conference on Italian American studies, I found myself unexpectedly learning more details about that troubled period of my mother's life: A group of us mingle in a hotel lobby, waiting to gather for dinner, and instead of passing the kind of small talk that most tired and hungry people might, another woman—a poet—and I find ourselves following a path from Louise DeSalvo's sister's suicide as one of the bases of DeSalvo's groundbreaking *Vertigo*, to the loss by suicide of the poet's female lover, to my mother's suicidal years. The poet, who is also from Philadelphia, knows my mother, and when we come to discuss her story, she asks me if my mother has ever told me "the story about the pie." She tells me that my mother once told her a story of how one day, as she was preparing to kill herself, the breadman rang the doorbell—and that this had saved her life. She bought a pie. She ate a piece of the pie. Soon my brothers and I came home from school and we finished the pie. "Maybe I shouldn't be telling you this," the friend, noticing discomfort on my face, says. And I say, "No, of course it's alright. My mother must have told me this story," I say, "and I forgot it." I really feel that there is nothing anyone can tell me about my mother that I don't already know, or they can't tell me anything that will shock me. But when I get home from the conference, I find myself thinking about this story as though the idea of my mother's possible suicide were new to me. I feel angry at the thought that she might have carried out the act, angry at the thought of what life would have been like for my brothers and me if our mother had taken herself out of our lives. It is a question that probably lies at the base of my identity. I never liked the breadman. He overcharged, and he showed up my inability to quickly calculate the change from his overpriced, stale confections. No doubt I want a story in which *I* ring the doorbell; *I* bring my mother a pie; *I* save my mother.

Before I see my mother's face, I hear her voice—laughing, talking, performing, reciting poetry, singing—she knows the words to each and every pop tune from the forties and fifties, she loves Italian arias, and church music remains meaningful to her even if she's left the church. Kaja Silverman's wonderful phrase "acoustic mirror" is the perfect image for what I want to say. If I had to describe my mother, I could say she's an artistic or a visual, a sensual, an intense, I could say she's a curious, an intelligent person. I could not say she is a "quiet" person. My mother is a verbal person, and her voice has a thousand different modulations for her various moods. My mother is a talker. Yet my mother rarely talked about growing up in poverty. And she certainly never laid her past like a burden on her children's shoulders by drawing attention to how much better things were for us. Outside of my mother's aversion to lentils, I did not know much about the experience and effects of poverty in the immigrant household. Or so I presumed, until I began to read in earnest the daily reflections that my grandfather penned in his shoe repair shop. Reading these pages, I don't merely hear or learn about those years, I *remember* them, as though I had experienced them. By this I mean that I recognize episodes, affects, and conditions as though they have already been transmitted to me, and I experience a welling up of feeling—pain, for example, finally attaches to its lost object and brings forth tears. It's as though my mother has told me all these many years about that poverty but only indirectly; or that she's told me in a separate language, the key to whose translation is the language of my grandfather's journal—half of which is written in a language that I never learned to read. Nevertheless, I need my grandfather to translate my mother's language for me—especially the language of her body or of her terror. In my grandfather's journals, I find some of the sociological bases of phobia and depression. I see how living with the threat of losing one's heat, water, electricity, and not having enough food to eat can easily engender states of terror.

The reader/scholar in me, of course, feels that she cannot solely rely on her grandfather's words for understanding what I might call the psychology of poverty—that is, the psychic states that poverty precipitates. So I attempt to do research as well. In all the annals of psychology that I consult, however, I can find nothing that links agoraphobia in any rigorous way with material conditions generally or with poverty in particular. Consulting psychology texts does not seem to help me as much as gardening manuals do in understanding my family. The emphases of all of the psychological treatises on agoraphobia that I find are on biologism through and through. On labeling and lumping diverse experience into mute categories. On talking about people's inner and outer lives as though they are talking about refrigerator parts. On not taking nuance, complex processes, or individual differences into account. When I write to a feminist psychologist friend of mine about this she tells me, "In earlier times they just called an agoraphobic a 'normal' woman who needs a man/protection from the dangerous public sphere. Did they ever think that the person from whom she needs most protection is the dangerous man (as [is] the case in one in two to three homes) in her life who claims to love her? Never. I don't know one woman who's suffered from agoraphobia who has also not had sexual/domestic violence in her history/present."

Jennifer's words help me to contemplate the sociological bases of my mother's agoraphobia and depression, as does a dream that my mother shares with me. I have read to her the opening pages of my book soon after writing them—the condensed version of the effects of my father's violence on me. The reading is not followed by our usual, lively conversation. There is silence now, and my mother tries to tell me that this is not how she remembers it. She's sorry, I think, about the sadness in these pages, and asks, "Was it really that bad? . . . I guess I didn't realize that Dad's violence had such a strong effect on you." I know that my mother knows how bad it was—

she's the one who wasn't able to leave the house for seven years—but it's hard to address the ghost of a past in the present, especially since that always means reaching back further to the ghost behind the ghost. We hang up, not having spoken about where my version of the story leaves us. I have a mild bout of not trusting the integrity of my memory, but continue writing nevertheless. The next day, my mother calls excited. She wants to tell me of a dream she had that night. It's so powerful and vivid that she has also typed it out:

Last night I dreamt that the mafia was out to kill my father; they were posted across the street from our house and we were laying low inside the house so they couldn't see us. At one point, we went up to a second floor balcony that consisted of a long and jagged slab; we thought that if we stood there we would be unseen. However, our shadows were visible on the ground before the assassins and so we had to move back. Besides, a child in our group kept leaning precariously over the side of the slab. Finally, my father arranged for an airplane to take some members of our family away from the danger zone. The airplane was in our living room and my father had to adjust the nose that held the propeller on to the plane. My mother and some others took off in it, the plane miniaturizing as it rose off the ground and pausing before the kitchen door (door between the dining room and kitchen) before it could leave. My father opened the door and off it went. I said to him, "How can a plane take off from a living room?" and he replied that all things were possible when one is trying to save a life. Meanwhile, I had school to attend and donned my brown Notre Dame High School for Girls uniform. I thought of how I was going to tell June Kohler, my best friend, about what was happening, that my family's lives were in constant threat from a gang of gun-wielders that lay in wait for us. Sud-

denly I was being told that I could tell no one. Absolutely, I must keep it to
myself or it would be worse for everyone. Now, I envisioned myself going to
school and lived in intense fear. How could I keep that to myself? And what
would happen to me when I walked out the door to go to school? My father
assured me they wouldn't kill me. I decided to flash my uniform as I walked
through the door so they'd know I was a young student and not kill me,
though I also realized I couldn't do anything about my body, which was not
a child's but a mature woman's. And as I was thinking of this, I awoke.

I know it can be dangerous to interpret other people's
dreams—especially if you then make the interpretation public. In that "Shakespeare and Psychology" course, I had used a
dream of my closest friend for our dream interpretation as-
signment, and when she found out that I did this, it almost destroyed our friendship. In white Western culture, dreams are
private affairs—they are ever only about the dreamer, and it's
most important, therefore, that the dreamer remain their pri-
mary interpreter. Dreams tend not, in this culture, to have a
prophetic or communal purpose, and thus there's a tendency
to think of the individual dreamer as owning the dream. But I
believe that my mother partly had this dream for me in order
to communicate something unsayable about the history of
fear and violence that we share. She calls to ask me what *I* think
the dream means. I tell her what's more important is what she
thinks the dream means. She claims ignorance. I say it seems
to be all about her one-time agoraphobia. She agrees, "Yes,"
she says, "oh, Mary, you're right." And then we move onto
other topics. My mother does not talk easily about those years,
so she gives me this dream in the form of a letter instead. I give

her a part of my book; she gives me a part of hers. I know without her saying it that my mother is letting me have this dream, her dream, to read. I am the family reader—it's how I show my love.

What I notice about the dream is that it's a dream that is also a memory. Certainly my mother's agoraphobia was partly an effect of my father's inability to nurture and, worse, his brutality, especially toward my brothers. But the dream suggests another earlier domestic space as backdrop to the one in which this violence occurred—the danger zone that my mother herself grew up in. Her own family is threatened in the dream by what can be seen as my father—the Sicilian side of the family, whether mafioso or not, the "mafia"—but this detail is the stuff of dream and not of memory. It suggests that the violence of poverty is hard to locate; the source of the harm produced by social systems in which some people are left to starve while others survive easily and plentifully, is never readily named, exposed, found out. Easier to represent it to oneself as a form of black-on-black violence.

My mother's dream is populated by powerful images. The family attempts to hide out on a "long and jagged slab"—a jetty, a plank, Italy itself? But they can't hide out here: their shadows are visible. The domicile has become Bentham's panopticon, an insidious prison architecture whose circular design coerces its prisoners into internalizing the surveilling eye. Each cell is lit by windows through which a guard standing in the central tower can read the prisoners' shadows; the prisoners can neither see one another nor the guard, and the guard needn't literally be present for the structure to do its work. As Foucault describes it in *Discipline and Punish*: "By the effect of backlighting, one can observe from the tower, standing out precisely against the light, the small captive shadows in the cells of the periphery. They are like so many cages, so many small theaters, in which each actor is alone, perfectly individualized and constantly visible." At the center of the dream, a plane lifts survivors out of a living room, and a typically cryptic sentence is spoken by my grandfather: "all things are possible when one is trying to save a life." Now the family appear as hostages, but who or what holds them? And why can the fact of their imprisonment not be shared even with one's closest friend? The command of silence is issued as though it's been translated from one language into another, from Italian into English? I can't, for example, help but notice how the qualifier seems so oddly placed: "*Absolutely*, I must keep it to myself." It's my grandfather, I decide, who has issued this command.

The dream ends with a sexualization of the family secret, of what's menacing the family, with the desire to tell now understood as a need to "flash." The innocent child body might protect one, but the desiring adult body will only lead to one's being found out. And this is a tragic end played out in real life when, as is so often the case, women living in already threatening situations are forced to replay rather than resist the threat across and through their own bodies: "I couldn't do anything about my body which was not a child's but a mature woman's." I couldn't do anything about my desiring and desirable body, about the need to connect to other people, about the drive to share, to tell, to know, to cease to keep the secret of my father and my family's suffering. My body would announce it if my words would not. My body would tell.

This is my analysis of the dream, but there are also my conscious projections into the dream. I decide, for example, that I might be the child in the group "who keeps leaning precariously over the side of the slab." My mother is concerned that my writing about my father's violence endangers the family. I also realize, though, that in telling my mother my version of what happened in our household, I've made her want to tell a best friend about what went on in hers. My writing may provoke fear, but it also rekindles desire. At another point in the dream, I feel sad. I feel that if the dream were *my* dream, my mother's brown school uniform would be a metonym for the brown jumper that she wore on our walks to the library, and I'd remember how much the sight of that woolen jumper warmed me at the same time that it didn't entirely protect my mother from her fear.

Most of us don't have access to the aura of our parents' childhoods, but my maternal grandfather's journal offers me that. My mother's dream, my grandfather's jottings, translate to me a theory of agoraphobia that unmoors it from a strictly private sphere. My mother's agoraphobia might be a sign that something terrible was happening in the immigrant household. To go outside would be to announce it, but its expression is prohibited. And it's not sexual abuse or domestic violence but some unnameable hurt experienced by the immigrant, her father, "the man who is not a man," that she witnesses or in some way "receives"—something that was understood to be dangerous to share with mainstream culture. The fear has to do with a fear of proclaiming, even through one's body if not through speech, and the phobia is about the compulsion to proclaim and the fear of homelessness attendant upon that. Her body would announce it if her words would not. Her body would tell.

If I add to this what I remember about the aftermath of my mother's agoraphobia, the theory gains another side. Once my mother started to go out again, strangers were drawn to confide in her their secrets and pain as well as their joy. Strangers with difficult stories to tell seemed to gravitate to my mother, as though she exuded the quality of a sympathetic listener or as though she were wearing a sign on her back that read "empath." This happened so often that I came to wonder if the anticipation of yet another unusually intimate encounter with a stranger was a factor in my mother's fear of leaving the house. The conversations would often end with the person looking me squarely in the eye and saying: "You have a wonderful mother." Then they'd look sorry to say good-bye, and I'd swear they'd seem as though they might want to reach into their pocket or purse to pay my mother for her public service. Encounters like this could occur anywhere, but they were bound to happen as we waited, after a mile walk from our house, on the commuter train platform at the Lansdowne station en route to Philadelphia or once we had boarded the train. One especially memorable meeting involved a woman who looked distressed, who looked, according to my mother, as though she were contemplating throwing herself in front of the train. I didn't notice this: to me she looked like any other commuter—fancy rain slicker, business suit beneath, coiffed hair. The woman started to weep silent tears, then turned in the direction of my mother and me. She told my mother that she was tremendously upset because she'd just been to the doctor and had found out that she was pregnant. But the child wasn't her husband's. The child belonged to a man she'd had an affair with during a period of months of separation from her husband. Now she was back with her husband, and she wanted to make it work. She couldn't pretend the baby was her husband's because she and he were white and the lover was black. She told my mother she saw no way out and that she wanted to kill herself. My mother took her out of earshot from me and spoke to her and held her for a very long time. The train arrived. We sat with her on the train. When we arrived in the Philadelphia underground station, my mother asked the woman if there were anyone she could call immediately or someone she could go to. The woman said there was someone she could call, and my mother made her promise as we left her that she wouldn't harm herself.

Such experiences with my mother in public make me wonder if agoraphobia is less a fear of the connections that the marketplace represents and more a fear of the knowledge that lack of connection or refusal of connection between people is the normal order of the day. Feeling claustrophobic on a subway car as an adult, I have found myself fantasizing that each person buried in her silent book might stand up and read aloud to us all. It would make the ride so much more interesting. If someone would just stand up and read aloud to the whole subway car, then, I know, I would feel less trapped.

CHAPTER 8

"Do Not Despair to the Point of Frustration"

Many years after my parents' divorce, my father and I write to each other about our gardens. It's the only thing we share, outside of bad posture. My father was never so much a father as he was a child who wielded more power than the real children in the house, and who waited impatiently for his children to grow up so that he himself could have a parent. The unspeakable circumstance surrounding his own birth was that his mother—tired out and nervous from childrearing and caretaking of male adults (including her mildly disabled brother)—tried to abort my father using a folk method that failed. Mother and child survived a difficult delivery on All Saints' Day in which my father emerged feet first.

My father and I have no way to talk to each other except through the garden. He sends me Italian sunflower seeds in a homemade envelope; he laments on a rare visit to him that we are unable, due to rain, to survey the garden; I tell him about my garden's toad; he tells me about the night creatures whose flashing coats and flashing eyes pass his garden's paths; he writes of finding wild tomatoes and wild rose bushes in his garden, and reminds me to find time to lift a leaf to see what lurks there. He can't give me his mother's recipe for escarole soup when I ask for it—he doesn't know it, and recommends Progresso. He can't tell me anything about his parents' trip from Sicily and suggests I ask his elder siblings. But in one letter, he finally gives me instructions on the garden:

June 16, 1991. Dear Mary: The "Global Warming Affect" has settled upon the borough of Darby with a vengeance. The season of Spring is only on the calendar. On the bright side, I am so glad you've started a garden. Now when I go out into mine I think more of you as we tend to each of our gems with "T. L. C." Tips = Mulch around established plants. It prevents weeds from growing, conserves moisture, saves work, and all the plants enjoy its benefits. They will reward you for it. Beware of certain plants that are better kept in the wild for they tend to be awful parasites. These being "Morning Glories," "Japanese Lanterns," and "Lilly of the Valley," to mention a few. I learned the hard way. I use leaves and garden debri for mulch. It's free. If you have room in an out of the way place, start a compost pile that can eventually be used for mulch and it will also enrich the soil. Do not over fertilize. Doing so causes flourishing leaves, and less flowers.

In a letter written a few years after this one, his directions are more obscure and harder to make out in their Gertrude Steinian syntax:

I feel flattered that you would seek advice on gardening from this humble amature. The only way I know of to learn which is which when trimming is by constant, daily observation of the plants progression, like the results of time lapse photography. But do not despair to the point of frustration.

Since I think of despair as the effect of frustration and not the other way around, I take a certain joy in walking through the door that my father's sentence seems to open. The dark underside to my father's hopefulness around the garden, though, are the stories he always also tells of vulnerability, the failure of camouflage, the difficulty of subterfuge. He finds an iridescent bug the likes of which he's never seen before. He's accidentally disturbed its hiding place or its nest; he's frightened it into flight. He's never seen anything like it: so well hidden, so colorful. And now before his very eyes, the bug is eaten by a blue jay that swoops and gobbles it flying by. There's as much pathos and uncertainty in my father's writing voice as there is laughter that makes me uncomfortable in the way he narrates that story. In other letters, he tells me, abstractly, of the importance of self-protection:

There has been some unpleasant live action among some underworld (some people call them Mafia) characters in South Philly lately which has included gunfire with killings and maiming among themselves. The latest being a window shattering shootout at the "Blue Moon Saloon" on tenth and Tasker. I do frequent the same vicinities, where these incidents have taken place as I travel to and fro in South Philly. I always keep my car doors locked and it's a good idea for all motorists to do the same. It's a shame but I guess we just have to be on guard at all times.

In the light of my father's gardening advice, in light of a latticework of fears that are laced beneath, I have dreams, I have visions. Falling to sleep, I'm thinking of my grandmother, my mother's mother, Rose. Calling on her. I want to dream of her. I dream of a two-liter bottle of water or seltzer that has roses on the label. It's a kind of rose water, and on the bottle are the words "a hereditary drink." But I realize in the dream even after finding the elixir that I will need more than this to find my way home, more than gardening concoctions to take me out or in. I have visions: of flowers that come to seem like bits of torn paper, the remnants of a fair. The traces of color left in the wake of a melancholy rainfall, waiting for wind to lift their blanket of light into the air, after the cars of the ferris wheel have come to a silent, perfect, menacing stop. Gardens are a terrible silence, I say, and I need words. And so it is in the direction of words that I will work to turn, ever heeding my father's topsy-turvy advice, a nosegay made of stems above and blooms below: "Do not despair to the point of frustration."

THREE

CHAPTER 9

Nothing to Confess

In the same attitude and around the same age in which I'd cut my curls, adaze and adoze before the TV set, I lay belly to rug with one hand down the front of my pedal pushers, the other twirling a stray coil of hair round and round my fingertips, when my mother happened upon me and said: "Mary! What are you doing? Have you ever seen me doing that?" I don't think I realized how ludicrous the question was until I was an adult. No, I hadn't ever seen Mom masturbating, but then masturbation was something one did in the self-enclosed, lambent space of television-gazing, and my mother rarely watched TV. My third-grade teacher, Sister Mary Conrad, spoke as though masturbation was only something men and boys, who were barbarians, did, and she'd rap each boy's hand while screeching disgustedly about his "sticky fingers." She had a special preoccupation with conjuring for us the image of female prostitutes—she'd ask us to picture their halter tops, miniskirts, and high-heeled shoes. Then, just as I was imagining riding off with them on the back of my motorcycle, a sound, like a cannon blast would issue from Sister's yardstick hitting the desk as she tried to convince us that if we ourselves wanted to join God and his heavenly angels in the next life, we would do best to wear our woolen school uniforms round the clock.

From about age eight to age sixteen, in those perilously "formative" years, when vampirism and werewolfism threaten to suit the face of one's emerging id just so, I was a supplicant at the altar of two major icons: the Blessed Virgin Mary and Batman and Robin. The figures who won my gaze were elaborately robed but mournful religious heroes, and stalwart men in tights, saviors in disguise, fairies.

Recently I rediscovered the three-volume gold Naugahyde-covered *Lives of the Saints* whose stories, names, and pictures gave shape to my childhood fantasies and fears. I shared with a friend some of the images that most obsessed me as a child: "Saint John in Boiling Oil": a naked John seated in a life-sized cauldron underscored by raging flames, turns his head to one side as a man with a pointed beard, pointed nose, pointed ears, pointed hair, and bulging buttocks pours a pot of hot oil on his head. "St. Engracia": in one hand she holds a spike—emblem of her torture—like a pencil; the other hand holds both of her breasts between the span of her thumb and pinky, while those same fingers press into the respective nipples. Her eyes roll heavenward; a translucent scarf like a death shroud dances around her neck. "The Devil and St. Wolfgang": the devil appears as a Martian (he's green), or, if you will, as a cross between a mammal and reptile (he has both hooves and scales, gills and lungs). Last but not least, a photograph, "The Severed Arm of St. Francis": mightily decayed flesh clings to the bones of what once were a living hand and forearm, now displayed in a specially shaped and specially lined casket made just for it. Though the art in the book was almost uniformly drawn from the oeuvre of accomplished painters—from Botticelli to Raphael, from El Greco to Velázquez—the images of the saints appear to me now as grotesque cartoons, and *The Lives of the Saints*, a comic book tabloid of bad art through the ages, an encyclopedia of suffering.

Talking with my friend about the television shows we consumed most heartily or dreamily as children, I mention that my mother forbade certain shows like *Gilligan's Island*, *The Brady Bunch*, and *The Partridge Family*. Though she did not censor TV outright, she made me feel that such shows were only amusing to the brain-dead, and to watch them was to enroll oneself willingly in the universal club of morons. *Star Trek*, I recall, was allowed because it resembled the parables of Jesus and *Lives of the Saints:* every episode had a moral. I don't recall my mother's assessment of *Batman and Robin*. That was a show that I seemed to indulge in secret, unbeknownst to all. To my friend who has just toured *The Lives of the Saints* with me, my story is absurd: "So you weren't allowed to watch *The Brady Bunch*, but this book was deemed appropriate for children?!"

Within the domain of faith, anything goes. The Confirmation ritual (one of the Seven Blessed Sacraments) trained me at age eight to think of myself as a transgressor. I whispered my sins into the priest's ear, but more important, I did penance for my sins, said my prayers, and asked forgiveness before the statue of the Blessed Virgin Mary. Mary stands, palms open to me, feet bared, body robed, head veiled, eyes sullen, in the left transept of our parish church—B. V. M.—so that if I stand in front of her, I can see the altar in a blurred periphery. I know that my head should bow in humility before this great woman, but I always find myself searching out her eyes. When I don't turn into a pillar of salt (my confusion of the act of curiosity with another biblical story), I continue to gaze. Her hands say I can come to her, her feet say she can get down and dirty, but her eyes report a mystery of sadness. None of the saints in this church ever smiles, and she is no exception. In fact, she's the model saint, the Saint of Saints.

Sometimes when I lift my unknowing eyes to her sad face, I read her sadness as a sign of the pity she feels for me for being yoked to her daughters' tutelage: the punishing Sisters of the Immaculate Heart. I think they are nothing like her, and I remark to myself even at this young age the contradictions between the way the sisters treat us—often via bodily harm—and the precepts of a faith based on forgiveness.

"Every day's a holiday with Mary," Dick Van Dyke had sung in a Disney musical I knew, and though he'd been singing of a real woman whom he loved, I applied the song to my Mary, the Blessed Virgin. The candles that were forever lit before her in our church led me to think of birthday parties, and I knew she was connected to a special, a "miraculous" birth. A consummation larger than life, one that did not require a man, marked her. And yet the celebration was tainted. On a walk to the candy store with my cousin, I whistle my heart out, until she tells me that, according to our grandmother Rose, "girls who whistle make the Blessed Mother cry." That the Blessed Mother *can't* cry, I always thought, was precisely the problem, or my problem with her statue. Her hurt remains as remote and as incurable (by me) as my mother's. The celebration is tainted because the real-life female followers of this woman lack significant power within the church. From a very young age I was aware of the nuns' diminished worth in the eyes of the church and in the eyes of their "brethren," the priests. The hierarchy was clear: the nuns punished us because the priests devalued them. But Mary again remained a mysterious alternative, and I couldn't believe that she cried when little girls whistled, that little tomboys made her sad.

There must be a link between prohibited sexuality and Catholicism because to be Catholic is to be defined by a coming-out story. Every ex-, lapsed, or still-practicing Catholic has one to tell, and I have seen such stories, however devoid of poetry, however banal, typically tinged with horror and humor, bind a group of strangers together like a charm. The Catholic coming-out story is characteristically one of humiliation and abjection; it is the storyteller's share in the cultivation of self-loathing and fear that his religious training bequeathed him. The Catholic coming-out story is equivalent to a sharing of stigmata: "Here's my wound, my battle scar, my badge," we seem to say, "Can you imagine that? Can you imagine I survived to tell the tale?"

It's the day after Halloween, All Saints' Day, a Catholic holy day, and I have gorged myself the preceding night with one too many Reese's Peanut Butter Cups. I'm in sixth grade, which means I am enduring the rite of passage through the disciplinary hoops of one of the harshest sisters, Sister Bernice. Sister Bernice has already drawn blood from me when, one day, making her rounds to inspect our math problems, she decides to poke the point of her pen into the top of my scalp in time with the rhythm of her sentence. Each jab is equivalent to a word: "I (jab) told (jab) you (jab) to (jab) write (jab) the (jab) problem (jab) out (jab) first (jab) before (jab) solving (jab) it (jab)."

"But I did, Sister! Here it is on the other page," and I show her through my crossed brow.

"Sorry," she says. "Sorry," and I remember bringing my hand to my head, and the horror and anger and fear when I see the blood from my head on my hands, the blood she has made me bleed. Wincing with pain, I cry silently as I continue to add the table of numbers on my page using the method she has taught me: "Six plus 7 equals 13, write the 3, carry the 1."

I didn't tell my mother because I was afraid she would complain, and I was convinced this would only make my life with Sister Bernice more miserable—she'd punish me more harshly for exposing her. I saw what happened when people's parents' got involved—the child's life with Sister became a living hell. It was maybe one or two o'clock in the afternoon in Sister Bernice's class on All Saints' Day and she was going over a catechism lesson. I remember we were learning the words for the various church dignitaries, constituencies, and hierarchies. The pope was different from a bishop who was different from a cardinal who was different from a priest, and the range of their jurisdiction had separate names. I felt a sick, gassy, diarrhea-like feeling, but I knew that lavatory time had already passed, and I knew we were expected "to go" only during designated times of the day. If you raised your hand in the middle of a lesson to ask to go (which I never, ever did), Sister would yell at or thrash you before letting you go, and sometimes she wouldn't let you go at all. Diarrhea doesn't allow for laborious decision making. Every now and then I looked in the direction of my best friend, and she looked back as if to say, "What? What is it?" I wanted to tell her how I felt, and to consult with her about whether I should ask to go to the bathroom, but before I knew it, all such agonizing was over and I had shit in spite of my best efforts at self-control. Horrified, I continued to pretend that nothing was wrong as Sister Bernice announced we should report to homeroom, pack our bags, and file into line for church. Today, a holy day, would be concluded with a visit to church. The stench emanating from the back of my wool uniform was unbearable; my homeroom classmates could smell it now, but the teacher distracted them from their search for the source by giving us instructions on the church service that was to follow.

Once in church, Sister Bernice somehow ended up sitting next to me. I could keep the smell under control so long as I didn't move, but moving from sitting to kneeling and from kneeling to standing unleashed a scent that "stunk to the high heavens," as Sister Mary Conrad used to say of marigolds. And with each movement, I looked either at Sister Bernice's face or at Eileen Hogan's, who sat on the other side of me. Eileen looked as though she wanted to vomit into her prayer book, but I could see that "Bernice," as we called her, had been more deeply affected. She looked woozy and gray, her senses were askew, the words of her prayer were a jumble, her ears hurt (she kept covering them). Every now and then, she would, wincingly, get out of the pew and walk a lap around the church. Secretly, I thought, I had achieved a small triumph, I had been getting back at her. I don't know what kept her from humiliating me further—she must not have been able to truly tell where the smell was coming from, and at the end of the longest church service of my life, I ran all the way home, crying all the way, home to my mother who showered and bathed me and helped me to feel less desperately alone.

I think that I came to believe after that incident that I had paid for the sin of overindulgence. It was the kind of warped stranglehold that Catholicism applied to desire. But Catholic ritual, its forms, its rhetorics, its images, visages, scents, and artifacts, its inability to console, even its punishing face *produced* sensuality and made certain powerful feelings emerge in bold relief. My teachers' presumably nondescript and generalized garb, for example, actually encouraged me to think more than I otherwise might about their bodies. I fantasized about the color of each sister's head of hair. Did her hair match her eyes? Was it long or short? Did she allow herself to see it for herself, or did she wear her veil round the clock? Did she stroke or comb it, or had she shaved her head bald? Later I discovered that truly beautiful women didn't need hair as a beautifying prop. This I learned when I saw on a talk show my heartthrob, Linda Carter—who played (rather poorly, but who cared?) Wonder Woman in the TV series—in a guise that had her hair plastered to her head. Her face was so strong and purely gorgeous, I thought, she didn't need a fancy hairstyle. Or maybe I could see her face now, just as I contemplated my sisters', because she had downplayed her hair. And the sisters' wimples made me wonder if it hurt their jaws to chew or talk; and a wisp of hair escaping from their veils onto their necks made me want to touch their necks; and the heavy cross that left an indentation on the part of their uniform that covered their breasts made me wish to lift the cross to kiss it. One nun had the habit of running her thumb and index finger inside the elastic cummerbund that was part of her uniform. Could I slip my hand inside and feel her stomach? Did her hand inside her waistband feel to her the way, on a winter's day, through a marble cold church service, I found my hands inside my muff?

No matter with what conviction I tell myself that I have left the precepts of Catholicism behind—for they were more harmful than helpful to me—Catholicism still asserts itself as the bedrock, perhaps the major tableau vivant of my desiring, and Christianity's visage seems ever to mediate my most intimate relationships with other people, and even my means of communicating with myself. It has left its indelible mark, and on some level I will never fully own the power and magic of its traces.

During my passionate (though unconsummated) love affair with Julia, I was inspired to compose a love poem a day, the nature of which I could stealthily hide through the use of the gender neutral pronoun, "you." Julia and I had intense, furtive talks in dark corners of the college library, and occasionally our pelvises would longingly touch then just as powerfully pull away from each other on a college dance floor. Unlike most students at the semirural liberal arts college I attended, Julia lived at home with her parents, and occasionally she would invite me over to listen to her play the piano—lying beneath the instrument, I would be George Sand to her Chopin. I could tell her mother didn't appreciate my visits, and I guessed there was something not "right" about our relationship in her mother's eyes: her mother knew something about our relationship that I only almost knew and wasn't fully willing to admit. I also knew that something "terrible" and inexpressible had happened at the college that Julia had been attending in Philadelphia, something so painful that Julia found herself living back home, something to do with another woman, and seduction, and betrayal, and theft of musical property, and the dread of an identity lost. Julia found refuge with her mother and sister in the born-again cause, so that by the time I met her, Christianity had become her newfound, sublimated way of seducing other women. I didn't want Christianity, but there it was, looming a distance between us at the same time that it set the only possible terms of our meeting. Because I loved her, I would attend the local fire-and-brimstone, Bible-thumping sessions run by a nondenominational "clergyman"—because I loved her, and because I would do anything to be in the presence of her and her sister's magnificent singing voices. Both Julia and Kate, her sister, were charismatic, in the genuine, not the dime-store religious version, of that word. Just as Kate reached the purest of heavenly heights with her soprano voice, Julia would lend a depth, making the sacred profane, and the profane sacred, making the room sultry, and making my body throb. This was always Julia's hope as a performer I think—to leave the audience breathless. Her sister blithely sang for Jesus: she didn't *mean* to touch anyone while she turned our bodies inside out.

After Julia and Kate had sung together, the preacher, taking advantage of our transported states, would take their place and command us to close our eyes (were mine opened or closed?) while he moved in abrupt bursts from grating whispers to quaking shouts about the power of Jeeeesus. The success of the event was gauged by the number of people who lifted their hands when he asked: "Have you let Jesus into your heart?" He would ask it over and over and over and over again as I scanned the room with my half-opened eyes to see that I was the only one still refusing to raise her hand. The one holding up the works. The one not willing to admit, as much as he implored and cajoled and convinced me there was no shame in admitting that the sisters' voices were Jesus', not their own. And I wanted to cry, "I have let Julia into my heart! I have let Kate into my heart! I have let the two most soulful sisters on the planet into my heart!" But I didn't because I was too afraid of what that meant—it was scarier even than Christianity had been, my longing to keep Julia and Kate in my heart forever. Julia and I would walk home together after these episodes—or rather, I would walk her to her house and then return alone to my dorm room, and wouldn't you know the air would always be damp after these gatherings and the ground matted with the faint sweetness of pink petals that had been shaken to the ground in the interlude. We would hug goodnight, a born-again Christian hug, but Julia would hold me just a little tighter until our stomachs were flush and our breasts were pressed into each other. Her strong, piano-player's hand always went right to my waist or the small of my back or reached between my shoulder blades, and I knew that wasn't about Jesus but I didn't have acceptable words for what it was, so I would go home and write a poem to that nebulous and nonexistent "you."

It would take another five years before I could admit that my "you" was a "she," before I could say that I love *her*, and I desire *her*, and I want *her*. That story is full of torture and torment, and, luckily for me, a nonhomophobic psychotherapist, and it culminates joyfully in the pursuit of a woman who was unlike anyone I had ever met, who would change my life forever, whose only traffic with religion was a healthy dose of Unitarianism in childhood, and who became my lifelong partner. But that's the coming-out story I'm reluctant to tell—it's the one we all already know. What seems more important to describe is the way that religious iconography continued to emerge when I least expected it, how it continued to compose powerful touch points of desire. My sexual awakening to lesbianism, as a presumed lifting of repression, wasn't, as one might suppose, ever simply equivalent to a shucking off of my Catholic training.

In college, I suffer nights where something inexplicable creeps over me and rides my body into dark passageways the whole night through. It begins disconnected to any thought as a stab or throb somewhere inside my brain, then proceeds to a feeling of chills, a racing pulse whipped on by the rider, and worst of all, an uncontrollable shaking from head to toe. These attacks send me to the bathroom a few times in the night. Years later I will recognize this feeling in a scene from Roman Polanski's *The Tenant*, as Mr. Trelkovsky crawls, breathless and sweating, along the hall of nightmares to the communal bathroom in his apartment house. I will barely be able to watch the film for my feeling of kinship with him. But now I try to exert a conscious effort over these episodes, only to get as far as asking myself, "What am I afraid of?" and answering, "I don't know." All that I can really do is wait until morning, when, luckily for me, the anxiety lifts, drifts, departs as inexplicably as it came. I share a room with one, sometimes two, other friends, but none of us knows about the personal torments the others may suffer. I assume this experience is peculiar to myself—I've never heard anyone talk about such feelings and I don't link what I'm experiencing to the panic I sometimes witnessed in my mother.

More regular than these evenings rocked in the arms of terror, though, are periods of unbidden, intrusive thoughts. My inner life is painfully interrupted—sometimes by images, sometimes words, less usually by violent, often grotesque sensations, sometimes sexual in content. In spite of the fact that this condition—what I come to call my "obsessions"—makes me feel as though I am destined for an insane asylum, makes me feel apart from myself, makes me feel as though underneath my kind facade I am a monster, makes me feel like crying, and makes me feel afraid, I share it with no one. The only consolation, if it can be called that, is that my "obsessions" form a recognizable repertoire, but the force of their repetition is almost daunting. When one day I learn about Tourette's syndrome, I think to myself, "I've got an internalized version of that." The quality of my schoolwork remains high in spite of my illness; my literature major helps me, through reading, to feel less ignorant and alone; my poetry writing helps me to transform, if by a fraction, some of my self-laceration. Dancing, however, functions almost alchemically as the one place where my obsessions cease to announce themselves. Either they are gone or they have joined hands with me—whatever the case, the dance floor is the only place in my world at this time where I feel truly free and truly alive.

My lover's maternal grandmother was a vaudeville dancer in the 1920s. She and her sister, with an act known as "the Mann Sisters," performed together on the national and international stage. Coloradans by birth, they assumed a trademark Western style of dance that included rope tricks and chaps made of brightly colored boas. Marriage brought their dancing careers and the travel it entailed to an end, but when my partner and I visited her grandmother, Marion, now stricken with Alzheimer's, in a nursing home out West, she seemed still steeped in the moment of her stage career. Painfully disconnected from so much that was local, including her granddaughter's name, she sang bars of vaudeville music for us in perfect pitch, demonstrated her favorite two-step, and studying our faces, asked almost suspiciously, "Do you girls dance?" Both of us had haircuts at that time that mimicked 1920s bobs, and I could only imagine that to Marion it might have seemed that she was addressing herself and her sister, now appearing fifty years after the day of their last dance. "Yes," Jean and I replied, "We dance. We love to dance." And it was true. Our relationship began on a dance floor, and as we approached middle age we continued to enjoy exhibitionistic flings and improvisatory trots on the dance floors of parties and bars.

It's hard to locate the precise origin of my unofficial career as a dancer, of the pleasure that it provided me, of its erotic life. On those rare occasions when my grandmother Rose had to watch me in my mother's absence, she and I would play a recording entitled, "Ding Dong Bell" over and over. I would dance to the songs that the schoolteacher narrator sang, and my grandmother would express amazement and joy. To be looked after and to be lovingly looked *at* collapsed in those episodes. I recall none of the songs on the record now, and I suspect they were tunes with fairy-tale lyrics or with instructions for being a good student that a child was expected to sing along to. I adapted instead a modern dance form to the John Cage–like starkness of the school mistress's tolling bell.

The rather unmelodic *Batman and Robin* theme song also inspired movement from me, and, clad in my pedal pushers and stocking feet, I'd usually begin each viewing of the show with a dance that consisted of running in place before the television screen. This was long before the days of aerobics, and my dance was not so marchlike as my description might suggest. Rather, my short limbs became long, loose, and lanky in this dance even if my head was trained forward in the position of a concerned crime-buster. I don't know whom I identified with more, Bruce Wayne or his "youthful ward," but I was especially drawn to the way Adam West's nipples poked through his nylon costume, and I gritted my teeth with Robin when, punching his fist into the palm of his hand, he'd yell, "POW!" in the same manner as the balletic gang members of *West Side Story*. In one episode, a Russian dignitary, suspecting that Batman and Robin are not human, asks them to reveal the bodies beneath their costumes. Batman explains that in order for them to do their jobs, their identities must remain obscure, while he assures her that "under this garb we are perfectly normal Americans." Under this garb, under the garb of the man with the painted-on eyebrows, I knew, was a man who was as queer as a two-dollar bill. As I came closer to pubesence, I began to watch men's wrestling matches on TV on the sly. Men in tights, holding each other, rubbing against each other, throwing each other about and even mock-hitting one another, filled me, in a way that is either deeply complicated or deeply primal, with what I will later know to call "orgasmic pleasure." (Their counterpart in my adult life is gay male leather porn.)

When I'm not watching men in tights, I'm in the basement of our row home imitating, by turns, Nancy Sinatra singing "These Boots Are Made for Walking" and "That Old Black Magic" or Janis Joplin singing something sweet, hard, and indecipherable. I bring my brother's guitar with me for these performances amid the dirty laundry, washtub, and cache of tools that my father uses to grumpily repair just about everything and nothing. I picture a future as a rock star. The pantsuit of my fantasies is a shimmering polyester turquoise with glitter appliques of which my audience is most appreciative.

Dancing is always unreserved, a form of drag racing, or of testing a limit, but when I lead my future partners—and I almost always prefer to lead—I do so in the light of a childhood game that had an unforeseen bloody ending. One of my Catholic school playmates and I occasionally played a game to shorten our walk home from school: one girl shut her eyes while the other pulled her by the hand over the broken pavement, over the Lot's weedy hill, and up the road to our houses. The pace of this game of abandon and trust was left up to the leader. One day as I led her fast and faster past the streaming cars and dusty goldenrod of Lansdowne Avenue, the two of us laughing as we went, my friend's temple struck the side of a wrought iron railing at the bottom of our street. Her eyes were shut, she had given herself to me, and I hadn't taken care. This seemed to be the only way I was able to read what happened. She didn't show anger but looked stunned at first and then afraid as we both, trying to deny the severity of the bruise, gasped before the blood that was trickling down her face from her eyebrow. I walked her to her house where her mother took over, took her to the hospital for a set of stitches. I sometimes bathed the scar over her eyebrow with my gaze but could never talk about how sorry I was. Nor did we ever resume our "game" after that. Maybe there is no getting beyond the purview of haunting injuries. I know I continued to fear that I might hurt someone in my quest for pleasure, that exuberance might lead to harm or accident: I feared throwing caution to the wind. I could only "let go" in the self-contained space of the dance floor, each time, perhaps, trying to make that early dance with Dana work out right.

In my imagination, the walls of our row home living room occasionally fall away, especially when I tumble and stretch across its gray rug in the manner of a dance that compels the body, Martha Graham–style, to hug the floor. I continue to remember our living room opening, when, later into the 1970s, as Disco Diva, I "take up" the entire dance floor. Dancing will become my most exuberant release as well as the safest way to know and communicate with other people erotically.

In the late sixties and early seventies, while my older brothers contemplated the Beatles' intelligent lyrics, while they aspired to perform the intricacies of jazz piano or the high art of classical guitar, I played and replayed my 45 rpm discs of songs like Paul Revere and the Raiders' "Let Me." "Let Me" was all beat and no melody, and the lyrics were poundingly simple: "Let me, let me, let me, baby don't you get me?" My predisposition for music like this marked me as the family member with the tinniest of ears. My brand of music, my brothers unhesitatingly informed me, was known as "bubblegum," and they offered macho analogies that didn't mean much to me: "As Yamaha motorcycles are to Harley Davidsons, bubblegum is to rock." Probably my predilection for bubblegum was the early warning sign that I would turn to discomania as a teenager and young adult. Though Disco draws me unto her, my interest in dancing knows no generic bounds, it is absolutely nonpurist and is marked by contradictions. Though my sense of timing as a musician—my grandfather had taught me mandolin in previous years—is practically nil, I seem to be able to invent dance steps that make my body synchronous with any beat. My taste in *dance* music is rangy—on the dance floor, all forms of music beckon my body to unbecome itself: jazz, folk, classical, swing, funk, jitterbug, or disco, each in their way make my world suddenly ebullient. Dancing is the one area of my life marked by iconoclasm. There is no rule, no order on the dance floor, I tell myself in those days, and yet as any former Disco Queen knows, the life of a diva is replete with ritual and form.

I had pretty much one disco outfit, which I wore like a school uniform. I cared for these garments, approached them, entered them like a priest his sacred robe, a toreador his suit of red and gold. The wide wrap-around skirt that tied at the waist, body suit, and diamond sleeved polyester blouse that also tied in a knot at the waist, were all a shade of maroon spilling toward plum. The pinnacle of lust and lushness that I hoped to achieve with the skirt (to her disco skirt, each dancer attaches a special dream) combined the work of particular dresses worn by Ginger Rogers and Cyd Charisse in their pairings with Fred Astaire. Ginger had one dress that kept spinning after her body had come to a complete stop. She's spinning, turn, turn, and turn again; she's left the ground, or so it seems, until the twirling resolves itself into the control her hips give her feet, solidly ground to a stop. The dress, however, keeps wrapping her body and drawing her close. It makes three more revolutions around her thighs and calves. When my disco dress continues to spin after I have stopped spinning, I dream I'm in Ginger's skin. No longer wrapping myself around her—though that's desirable too—I *am* her, and the erotic spectacle, I imagine, excites those watching what the dress can do.

In my incarnation as Cyd Charisse, oh dream of dreams, the skirt becomes the bright red sequined dress with which she slays Fred Astaire in a dance sequence that brings Minnelli's *Bandwagon* to a close: "Girl Hunt: A Murder Mystery in Jazz." Charisse, perched, sprawlingly, on a bar stool, chest open, legs crossed, breathes heavily beneath a high-fashioned trench coat as detective Astaire approaches her. She whips off the coat, and thus begins a battle between her red and his white suit, her high-heeled and his wing-tipped shoes. Charisse's dress has a middle panel that's been cut out from the sides of the dress, and at one devastatingly sexy point, she takes the panel firmly in her right hand and winds it in circles in front of her while Astaire freezes, hands off, to one side. Charisse "works" that central panel of her dress in a gesture that combines the snap of a rope trick with the steady writhe of a snake charmer. If the women in film noir could dance, surely this is what they'd do. This model for my own moves, my own fantasies, is a knockdown, drag-out dance, or rather, an immensely elegant fight that says dancing is more about vying for the territory of the body than about anything else.

The dancing that happened once a week at the one nonfraternity social space at the college I attended always began this way: once the DJ had decided that enough people had gathered and that the temperature was ready to rise, he or she would give my male partner and me the cue to get the dancing started. Sometimes we would walk hand in hand to the center of the dance floor and strike a statuesque pose before bursting into movement. In even more dramatic moods, each of us would enter the floor from a different place, and dance a separate sampler until we nearly accidentally found each other.

The dance floor was our proscenium; its ground, our ice. My partner is a tall, blonde, sensuous man who swishes. By day, he dresses like a Beat poet—a black turtleneck dominates his wardrobe, and a gold necklace dominates his sweaters, which sport a tiny gold pin, emblem of its wearer's high school drama club. By day he dresses like a Beat poet, but he's too clean to be Beat, and the tight white jeans he wears to dance suit him better. We met in English class where he and I were the only ones to speak in the presence of the most intimidating professor—an Indian Anglophile whom we uncritically adored. I usually vehemently disagreed with Matthew's interpretation of the literature we read, and out of this, our friendship bloomed. Our dance, all dips and hips, is a game of trust: I fall backward and he catches me; he looks ceilingward, and I temporarily become his feet. We both approach each other from behind, and enjoy the surprise. We are not romantically interested in each other, but once a week we transfuse body to body. Each of us is a closeted queen except on Saturday nights, our partnership, a meeting of intimate contours, a scream.

Dancing, even in what are assumed to be heterosexual spaces, does take me to other gay people, including the woman I come to spend my life with. Our courtship begins on a dance floor and the dance does not immediately lead to the presumably safe and private preserve of the bedroom. It leads to sex in the public sphere, where all sex really takes place, and in our case, as an enactment of the risk of our acts of love at home or abroad. We have sex in a library study carrel, sex in the corner of a lesbian bar, sex in the bathroom stall of a straight bar, sex in our shared graduate student offices, sex on a Greyhound en route to Toronto, sex in a '67 Plymouth Valiant on a blustery Buffalo street.

By the time I meet her, I have been getting help for my anxiety attacks, help to reach the inner voices I've cut off from myself, help to defuse my inner minefields, false alarms, all. I have started to see the analyst ostensibly because of a pattern I've noticed of being drawn to other women and them to me. In the most recent episode, post–college graduation, a new colleague at the high school where I am teaching promises to "show me the ropes." She's a woman twice my age, she's possessive and controlling, most of all she's convincing, and before I know it I'm kissing her against my will. But in the first session with the analyst, this is not what I talk about. I share with him instead my more terrifying secret, the painful monotony that I have shared with no one, of my daily, inner torment. I cry so many tears in that first session that there hardly seems room for words. The analyst listens, he supplies a tissue rather than a penance, he asks if I'd like to come again.

His office is fortuitously located in a basement suite across from Swarthmore College. The subterranean locale lends itself to excavation, and the proximity of the private college that was beyond my working-class reach brings back at least one major source of my disunion with myself when I realize the voices are in part ventriloquized by class-bound demons— those who would have me believe I didn't belong where I was, didn't deserve where I was going—not with a background like mine. When I gather the gumption to go to graduate school, I continue to telegraph to my underground correspondent: I do analysis by phone and by mail. Dancing, with each bend, turn, swoop, and fall continues to encourage me to seek, and to open. It's the early eighties and the glitter of the disco ball has faded, but when my newfound female partner reaches for my waist, I still record the questions that excite me there of trust, of closeness, of freedom or flight, matters of territory and quest—I'll take you there, let me take you there—that circus of lights inspired. I walk a tightrope; she mounts a trapeze. I want our fingertips to meet. When she takes me in her hand, I sleep better. I sleep the deepest nights I know. I whisper to myself a mantra: "Sleep, O gentle sleep."

"You really want this woman, don't you?" my analyst asks. And I reply, "Yes."

You are theatrically correct / but it is your / natural beauty / that makes me tremble

FROM "FOR MY FRIEND WHO IS A DANCER," A POEM BY ROSEMARY PETRACCA CAPPELLO FOR JERRY ROGERS

When my mother saw how much I loved to dance as a child, she suggested that she could enroll me in a class for formal lessons, ballet to be exact. But I knew that a tutu could do no more than grotesquely embellish the moves I improvised to "Ding Dong Bell" and "Batman." I always felt it was a look that my mother was after—she wanted to see me in a tutu, but I turned away from her or twisted my small foot into the ground and whispered an embarrassed, "Naw, I *don't* think so," whenever she brought up the prospect. For all I knew, formal dance training, ballet in particular, was the opposite of the rough and tumble, anything goes choreography for tomboys I thought I was inventing. I did not imagine finding kin in the halls where such discipline—another form of Catholic school?—occurred.

In college, I enroll in a class called "Modern Dance." I have only just discovered that formal dance outside of ballet exists, and I assume with a title like "Modern" that this course will provide the medium for my untrained dancing impulses. The teacher is a blunt, sturdy woman who makes of her body a complex telegraphy as she cuts across the mirrored room a series of jags, dashes, and dots to open each class. What I learn in this class is that I appear to be congenitally unable to follow directions, and that, though I fancied myself an athlete, I am hopelessly stiff and out of shape. I reject the importance of learning and following steps; I'm not ready for discipline in this area of my life, though I fall in love with the lives of other dancers, especially Isadora Duncan. I stink as a trained dancer, but the teacher relies on me for choreography ideas. "Improvise on this," she instructs me, and I become the primitive influence for the genius at work. She watches me, she contemplates me, and then she designs a step from what she's seen that she trains the two real dancers in the class to carry out.

The two real dancers are always already in the dance studio when the gaggle of misshapen others, about ten in all, myself included, arrive. One of them is a dark-haired, perfectly proportioned woman whose face is made up like an opera star's. She cocks her head toward the mirror as she bends her elastic torso over her left leg. She's wearing leg warmers. The other is an otherworldly creature, a man, I think, or maybe not, neither man nor woman, whose lithe, blonde figure, garnished in shades of pink, performs a stretch seemingly outside the rules of anatomy. He sits on the ground facing forward with one leg spread to the left of him along the horizontal line of the room; the other he has made perfectly flush with the wall to his right at a ninety degree angle. He has made of himself a compass. He has trained the effort of his being toward purity of line. He makes the slack-shouldered group of us, arrayed in various shades of baggy sweatpants, gasp.

The rest of us are there to fulfill a gym requirement, but these two are wrestling with the demands of art. The woman studies and performs as though we are not in the room with her; the man, for some reason, picks me out. Or is it I who have picked him out? Of all the people in the class, he's the one with whom I make eye contact, the one I am drawn to, the one who asks me one day if I'd like to walk home with him after class. His walk is swift and turned-out; I bob, jauntily. I'm uncertain of whether it's wise to leave the confines of the college campus with a stranger, but I am charmed by the combination of his delicacy and confidence: he knows where he's taking me; he knows why; he knows we're a match meant to happen, but of course. Getting to know him doesn't happen in stages, but all at once. He doesn't have time to wade through small talk or slow walks in the park: he brings me to the heart of matters.

We have to tiptoe into his house, he explains, because Katie mustn't know he's been out. Katie sleeps sitting up, covered in shawls, in a wheelchair in the center of the living room. A cat slinks by. "I have to be here for her," he explains, "but I'd go crazy if I didn't leave the house sometimes." Jerry, I now learn, is not a college student like myself, though he is my age. Jerry is Katie's live-in nurse. She's had a severely debilitating stroke, and she's hired Jerry to care for her. He bathes and feeds her; he entertains and reads to her; he cleans her house; he grooms her cat; he changes the bedpan, or he lifts her onto the toilet when she is able to move; he cooks for them both. In return, he gets room and board. "Room" is a tiny square that Jerry has fashioned into a world away from the world, room enough for a mirrored wall to dance before, a small personal library of dance and theater books, a poster of Gelsey Kirkland, a photo of his deceased mother, a cot to sleep on, a bedside table to hold his journal. Jerry grew up in some part of Pennsylvania not far from Carlisle, where we are, some place with a name like Sunnydale, where he dropped out of high school because he couldn't survive the ridicule—he shows me the town on the map—where his identical twin brother disowned him, as did his father, and then his sister. He longs to be a ballet dancer, he tells me, to dance *en pointe*.

Jerry isn't trained as a nurse, and I don't know how Katie has found him, nor why she is expecting him to sacrifice his life to her. He's grateful to her, I know, for the closet filled to the brim with costumes from her theater days that she allows him to wear, and for the sewing room adjacent to his bedroom that he now has taken over. "I'm a self-taught seamstress," he tells me, offhandedly, and then suggests we retire to the kitchen for some graham crackers and tea. On paper, we are both nineteen years old, but in my mind's eye, he is eons older than I am, and I go to him as to an elder for the wisdom of experience that he imparts.

On one occasion early in our relationship, when Jerry has invited me to tea, a woman answers his door. She's dressed in a Victorian skirt, blouse, and hat. Her hair is chocolate, her lips a subdued orange, and the narrow, button-up shoes she is wearing accentuate her ankles. She rushes around Jerry's house with a joy overbrimming, until we sit down for tea. Now she talks slowly as though there is much to say and more to think about. Not only does Jerry appear not to be at home today, but Katie is nowhere within earshot. Perhaps her relative has come to take her to one of her rare doctor's appointments, or maybe Jerry has relegated her to the basement while this meeting takes place. The woman talks about how hard it is to be a woman, a *real* woman these days, and of how she couldn't *buy* the clothes she fantasizes making in her head, and then she pauses to water the geraniums before taking her place again in the seat across from me, the two of us companionate, in the rowboat of our wide silence. "Drink, drink up," she commands, "you can't stop eating because of the state of things," as I sit staring, aware as never before of the doggy threads I'm decked out in. I feel in that instant that my sex lies fallow, my body unexplored. I am suddenly embarrassed. My ripped and dirty sneakers and my overly large sweatshirt—this is how I dress for school. Where was the skin that my intelligence could luxuriate in? If I shed these clothes, what would I choose in their place? And what of longing? I didn't want my Victorian companion, but I wanted her self-knowledge. What she had to know to appear before me this way was more detailed than anything I could claim to have studied up to then.

The course that Jerry and I are in together culminates in a public performance that makes me proud to know Jerry and despairing of my own possible entrance into the world of modern dance. My role is to perch as one of three Grecian urns, costumed in a nude leotard, candle in hand behind a gauze curtain. Jerry, the teacher, and the other trained dancer perform the meat of the dance center stage. Jerry's costume—a tight-fitting body suit—is the color of my disco skirt, and he astonishes the audience with the abstract reach of his limbs, his embodiment, *en pointe*, of sublimity. Jerry should really be paid for this performance, but the teacher no doubt assumes she's paid him by letting him attend the class free of charge. Just as the relative of Katie's who would check in on her once a month gave Jerry the impression they were doing him a favor by letting him take care of Katie round the clock, for who else would let a high school dropout, freak like him work for them? The world was a dangerous place for Jerry—this we all knew—and these people pretended to protect him.

I manage to have a sense of humor about my debut as Grecian urn, though I resolve not to enroll in any more dance classes. At the end of the performance, I invite Jerry to celebrate by dancing at my disco spot on campus. By the time Jerry arrives, Matthew and I have wreaked havoc on the dance floor, but I find a third and fourth wind to meet this dream: to have the honor of dancing with Jerry as myself, as it were. From the waist down, in jeans and ankle-high hush puppies, Jerry looks like a businessman at leisure; from the waist up, he looks like a woman on the make—he's wearing a white shirt that, like mine, is knotted at the waist, but somehow his cleavage is more convincing. My moves are too fast and unpredictable to follow, he says, too much my own. Jerry stands in one place upending his hips; I, as usual, concentrate on unraveling the space between the four corners of the dance floor, but when we try momentarily to dance *together*, it's a serious affair whose theme seems to be resoluteness. Jerry is all bone, I realize when I touch him, and his bones announce the fact over and again that he is here, that he is standing. As for me, I'm a little more like putty, but I am as sure that I have something, through dancing, to shape and to say.

Jerry tells me things about myself and my friends, most of which I only half hear, much of which I feel I can take or leave. My disco partner is, no doubt about it, he says, gay—and haven't I considered that I'm probably a lesbian? All of these pronouncements are within the realm of risky possibility and I even encourage such soothsaying on Jerry's part, except on the occasion of one birthday when he goes too far for my inflexible limbs to reach. His gift is enclosed in an envelope. The penmanship on the stiff card is measured like the script on a formal invitation, but there is nothing quiet about the promise that the words propose. It reads: "This entitles the bearer to one Fred Astaire jacket made to order. Happy Birthday, Mary! Love, Jerry." The year before that, on my twenty-first birthday, he had given me a copy of a treasured book from his small library, *Ballet Studio*, with an inscription that I liked just fine: "To 'Fred Astaire' and her cultivated elegance out on the

Dance Floor. You're the Tops! 'Gelsey Kirkland'"; on other occasions, flabbergasted by the shield of my workaholism, he brings me "autumn in a paper bag," as he calls it. "If you can't take a walk, then I'll bring autumn *to* you," and he hands me a bag filled with leaves and feathers and party-colored stones, and the dried and spherical labyrinths that the trees have shed. He has sewn dolls for my friends and me. Each doll is the size of a small cat and just as full of distinctly haunting personality. But this year's offer of the jacket has touched a nerve. I love the woman in Jerry; he acknowledges the queen inside my tomboy body. But for him also to have confirmed my desire to be Fred Astaire is beyond the realm of my own self-acceptance. Unable to celebrate that with him, I reject his gift. I don't remember if I was stupid enough to tell him what I was thinking: "You might want to dress as a woman, you might want even to be a woman, and I can accept that. But don't then suppose that I must want to dress like a man, or that I might want to be a man. Because I don't. I don't. I don't." Let's just say that in a form that I have since hidden from myself, I gave him the message that he must not make the jacket for me, that I did not want this gift. Perhaps it was equivalent to straight people's saying that homosexuality was ok so long as they didn't have to sit next to it in the park. Beneath my rejection was no doubt a longed-for assurance: "I'm normal, Jerry. It's you who are not."

Before my college graduation ceremony, while the other parents gather at the president's house for a garden party, my mother and I are poised on the edge of two small, cushioned stools in Jerry's narrow bedroom waiting for him to begin his performance. Jerry has been working on this dance for months, and we are the first, possibly the only ones, to see it. He's dancing solo to a suite from Prokofiev's *Romeo and Juliet* as Juliet. Her hair is long and dark against the light blue chiffon of her dress and white toe shoes. I had never quite seen anyone make a room become them like this, except perhaps my mother. Jerry's body, the dress he made for it, the expression he gave his face and hands, the bold and strenuous exaltation of his limbs, shaded and brightened and rocked the room down to a steady standstill. How strange for my college career to culminate with my teacher dancing for me. It seemed it should have been the other way around.

After graduation, Jerry disappears and reappears in my life, always a palpable presence and absence. I light out for the territory of teaching, but his letters to me seem more and more dispirited. He is family-less, jobless when Katie dies, moneyless, and he lives in a world where the only medium for his form of dance is caricature—he refuses, he tells me, to join the Trocaderros. He never puts it to me this way, but I should understand that he is also homeless. He has been evaluated at Johns Hopkins for a trial sex change, but what keeps him from pursuing it is the knowledge that the softening of his muscles will leave him unable to dance, certainly unable to dance *en pointe*.

He begins to call me again when I'm in graduate school, the remote distance of Florida to Buffalo. He tells me he fears that someone will kill him someday for who he is. He is hungry, but has no appetite. He also pretends, between telling me these feelings, to be upbeat. One day, he calls me with a surprise. "Guess where I'm moving to?" he asks. "You won't believe it, but I'm moving to Buffalo." And he asks if he can stay with me until he finds a place of his own. I say yes without checking in with my roommates. Of course, a week's visit from a friend will be ok. Jerry arrives with all he owns in a duffel bag, and a transparent story about having had all of his money stolen on the bus ride along the way. A week stretches into two weeks and then four. My roommates didn't anticipate another roommate even if this one does insist on cooking meat loaf once a week and ironing our shirts until they cease to look like the rags that they are. There's really not enough room in our apartment for the choreography he has composed to accompany the drag performances he has begun to work on, and when one evening he momentarily breaks the heartthrobbing pace of his show by accidentally kicking a lamp out, I think of how true it is that Jerry's stage needs to be the world, and not, as it has always been, bare, domestic spaces with the shades drawn. Jerry is too intellectually taxing for any of us, and too emotionally demanding. The strains that graduate school has placed on our individual egos are immense. What Jerry needs, no one of us has to give. Jerry must go.

This time when Jerry disappears, he takes off with the short and slinky silver-sheened evening dress that I purchased for myself in a thrift shop. Another friend complains that he hasn't returned her iron, a rather expensive deluxe model. Six months later, when I hear from him again, he tells me he has good news and bad news to share: the bad news is that he has full-blown AIDS, but he tries to explain when he tells me this that AIDS does not scare him because he feels he has lived with and through worse; the good news is that he's found a place to live: in the home of a practicing Catholic priest who is gay, and who cares for men who are HIV positive, in Harrisburg, PA.

The Catholic Church. There it was again: At the beginning of every dance. In the middle of every dance. At the end of every dance. Why did it take a priest to care for Jerry in a way his friends could not? Father Sandy's example certainly couldn't make me convert back, but I thought of his individual person as a miracle, and I was painfully aware that the church was helping Jerry now in a way the gay community never had. And yet maybe the "church" would only recognize him now that he was dying, whereas Father Sandy was committed to Jerry's continued life.

Living inside some version of Catholicism, Jerry tells me he feels freer than he ever has before. He has taken now to what he calls "ecclesiastical sewing"—finally, the Catholic altar seems the place to accommodate his extravagant creations:

The stole I made for Father for Christmas turned out beautifully. In fact, a Fellow Deacon of the church saw it and was very impressed by it. He priced it at $300 if someone was to buy it from a Catholic supply shop. It did not cost me near $300 needless to say. The stole's reception was so great that it made me decide to continue ecclesiastical sewing. As you can see Lot's of things are going on, so I'm fairly busy and keeping myself up. I'll just be glad when my Disability comes through and I have money again.

Folded within this letter are several painstakingly transcribed pages of Jerry's latest plan. The words are guided with the care it takes to thread a bobbin and sew a straight line, and

I picture these pages moving from Jerry to me in the way a favorite fabric might glide through the machine, beneath his hands, and into mine. Is he entrusting me with the map to his desire? Or is the whole thing a joke? Maybe there was a combination of the two in his idea of the cloistered dancer, the dancer turned nun:

I am working on my own Rule of Life for my own order of nuns (I'm the only one in my order, so I'm also Mother Superior at the Same time) and It's called the Gay Sisters of Ordinary Time. Sometime after the first of the new year I will start living my Rule, But I don't have it completed yet. I'm not planning on wearing a old fashion Habit. Although I would Love to. It's simply just too complicated to dress like that and still get around and things done. I'm enclosing the Beginning part of my Rule for you to read. Let me know what you think. Since I've always wanted to be a Nun ever since I was small, I thought this is the perfect solution.

GAY SISTERS OF ORDINARY TIME: RULE OF LIFE

OUR NAME   *Our Sisterhood, Known as the Gay Sisters of Ordinary Time, is based on our Love of Jesus Christ, and our loved ones through ordinary every day life. By following the examples of our Lord and his Mother, We Strive to Love God with all our heart and follow his teachings. We try not to draw attention to ourselves or our work, But go quietly along our way totally surrendering ourselves to God's will and what the day has to offer. Above all, we embrace our nor-*

mal everyday Lives and through service to our Loved ones,
neighbors and church, Strive to attain the Christian Ideal.
We Thank God and praise him for making us everyday nor-
mal people, for in this we can best accomplish our calling.

OUR WORK   *Our work is simply everyday Life. We try to keep the Lord*
present in all we do. The aim of our day is to become quietly,
But constantly aware of our relationship to God, not in
panic or praise or sudden trial, But all all times. By
employing the Day to remind us of God, we may use those
common Tasks that arise in our daily Grind. Some are
pleasant and anticipated, some routine, others, sudden, But
all are done with the assurance that God's presence is near
and that his Love is all around us. We Think of Mary and
Jesus often, and try to pattern our Daily lives after theirs.

I don't know whether Jerry improvised on an existent guide-
book for nuns, or whether he mastered the rhetoric of a religious ruler by listening carefully to the way the clergy of his
new community used words. There's a beautiful chaplet in
these pages, a liturgical ode wrought with conviction, but the
refrain of God grant me normality in the everyday, ordinary
nature of who I am—the longing expressed here to be blotted
out and in that erasure, recognized, rather than to be loved for
the divinely queer person that he was—bereaves me. I cannot
find what is "gay" about the sisters of his order, except the desire to reside this side of alienation. Jerry, nevertheless, never
descended into the colorless realms of normality.

On a rainy July day in 1990, Father Sandy called to tell me

that Jerry had died. By the measure of "ordinary time," Jerry was barely thirty years old. The priest treated my mother and me as next of kin as he explained to me that we were the only people whom Jerry asked to be notified of his death outside of the new community he had formed in Harrisburg. There was static on the line as though the air could not reckon with a dancer's departure, and through the added noise of my tears, I had to strain to hear the priest's soft voice. He told me that Jerry, no longer able to move, called to him from the bottom of a staircase and of how he carried him up the stairs and to the bed in which he died.

In the ensuing years, in the 1990s, Jean and I like to throw combination dance/costume parties. One year, she's Harpo and I'm the Fairy Godfather; another year, she dresses as Emma Peel from the Avengers and I come as Zorro. Each year I really wish to dress as Fred Astaire. But how does one dress as Fred Astaire? I could never get my face and hair to look like his, and a tux alone would not suggest his persona. I once had a dream that I danced with Fred Astaire. It felt so real and rare that I woke up smiling. But I could never *be* Fred Astaire because that, of course, would require that I have a custom-made "Fred Astaire jacket." I cannot dance as Fred Astaire because when the opportunity was granted me, I did not take the risk. Or so I sulk, until Jerry appears before me, grinning, mocking my self-seriousness. He slays me in a dress that is the color of the Ace of Diamonds. He challenges me to match his delicacy but to do so in the body of a man, for what could be more beautiful? Bringing my hand to his extraordinary waist, guiding my hand past his half-revealed shoulder, he smiles toward the audience; under his breath, he commands me to "face the music, and dance."

We live in a culture that craves deterministic narratives, revelations, clues to sexuality's forbidden secret, simple explanations for complex desires. I'll never forget how my group of peers and I responded when a fellow academic was arrested for making obscene phone calls to twelve-year-old girls in his neighborhood. Almost instantaneously, each of us found a detail, a remembered look or conversation, a habit, either real or imagined, that accounted for his "deviance." If only we had access to his handwriting, his physiognomy, or the bumps on his head—then we'd most surely have been able to detect the inborn sign for his lascivious behavior. We retold the story that we'd originally made for him so that its parts would now add up to the criminal, the perverse, and most important, the "not us." The way that we made him make sense conformed to cultural practices we were well-trained in: simpleminded mastery and estrangement.

Our friend—but had he ever been our friend?—this man, his behavior, was, in its victimization of children, yes, unacceptable. Equally troubling were the lengths we went to keep him from the zone of our own aggressive and desiring impulses, the formulae we invent to make a desiring subject work out right or wrong, normal or perverse, criminal or sane, American or un-American, fit or unfit. Such scripts, as I know all too well, would in fact equate behavior that victimizes children with consensual sex between adults. But maybe it's the equation—its marginalization of me—that makes me want to find a however uncomfortable point of identification with this man rather than to pretend that he, unlike the rest of us, is wholly legible, wholly knowable, thoroughly not me. Marginalization can be a gift if put to such uses.

I loved James Baldwin's sentiment: that no one had the right to tell you whom to love. Because no one knew enough about it. Mostly what I knew about it was that it appeared where people least expected it—that lesbianism was always there even as its presumably heterosexual makers and participants pretended not to see it. A queer sexuality was forming, reforming—try, and try again—before the altars of the Catholic church that was the medium for my ethnic group's sense of the sacred and profane; before the television set that they hoped would help them assimilate; and in the face of their reticence and fear about expressing themselves in a foreign land, a foreign tongue; in the space of their enforced silence, queerness rang out. Like all desire, its formation was as much about pain as it was about pleasure, but I could never find a day when it wasn't a cause for celebration. I offer no explanations for it, but, more truly I hope, a description of desire's eyes: of the faces in my life that looked in my direction and made me want them, and the faces that made me loathe myself for wanting them, and the faces that told me I, too, could make, was worthy, of love.

"What are you thinking?" "What are you feeling?" "Give, give it, give it to us, give it up." "When did you know you were gay?" "How did this happen?" "Why?" My Italian

American family's questions are the same as anyone else's, though perhaps they are asked with more volume and insistence. But I have nothing to give up. I have no secret. I have nothing to confess. Only the glorious and painful models that I studied, and loved, and imitated. What I was given is what I have to give. Lesbianism was bequeathed me—it was my Italian/American family's, nearly silenced, resistance.

However well I try to place it, "my lesbianism" insists on returning to the unarticulated space between my maternal and paternal legacies. Rather than having emerged, in true Oedipal fashion, out of an identification with one parent and disavowal of the other, my willingness to inhabit a space of transgressive pleasure found its impetus in the unresolved area of desire/lack that was the space between Anglo ideals and Italian realities. In "becoming queer," I was becoming what my Italian American forebears denied about themselves even as they provided the example. In becoming queer, I see myself as having made something wonderful out of an Italian American fabric, the Italian American weavers of which were too ready and willing to discard.

For the lesbian in me is the grandmother who as a child jumped rope with such intense and rapid, with such forceful pleasure that her mother was driven to threaten her with stories of "the little girl who died from jumping rope"; she is the grandmother who made the mistake of singing in the Catholic schoolroom "Holy Roller" songs that she had learned on North Philadelphian street corners—songs with titles like "Sail On," and "Brighten the Corner Where You Are"; she is the mother who was ostracized from the local town meetings for speaking out against racism and who fought the church fathers with poetry; she is the daily bliss of generations of these mothers combing their daughters' curls; she's Great-Uncle "Diamond" who never left his mother, her grocery store, but who, during Lent, amid the abstaining stench of codfish soaking in their wooden barrels, manufactured ecstasy—my first pineapple sundae; she's Great-Aunt Mary who the family refused to see for many years because she married a black man (I remember studying a photo of Aunt Mary, in which she sits on the floor and draws one knee playfully up to her chest; she's wearing short hair and pants); she's her father before he got married, gallivanting with his gay friend, Alfonso; she's the love the father could not express toward Alfonso and so he made Alfonso the godfather of his first son and then beat the son repeatedly; she's the grandfather who taught her, the smallest and a girl, to play duets with him on mandolin; she's the grandfather who guided viny tendrils, then roamed his garden in silence; she's the aunt who entered the convent without giving up the world. When Sister B. brought home a secular girlfriend, the family said nothing about their holding hands at the dinner table, nothing about the girlfriend bestowing the aunt with lavish gifts; but when Sister B.'s real sister died, they—the alcoholic Anglo husbands being most vehement on this score—denied her girlfriend the privilege of viewing the corpse. I remember seeing the girlfriend, whose toughness I enjoyed, weeping.

It has been twenty-two years since my last confession, and these are my sins:

I let a woman who had been spared religious discipline

open the envelope of my desire, then read my body through whole languorous, undying afternoons. My favorite English professor was an Arab Sufist who, rather than order books for the class, told us to sit silently, then wait for a door to open. I entrusted my sorrow weekly to a Jewish psychoanalyst. Whenever I was alone, I worked rather than played with myself. I feared dwelling too long with Happiness—she might want me to wear her clothes. I translated my anger into an indecipherable language then buried it in a box marked EXPLOSIVES — DO NOT HANDLE OR OTHERWISE ATTEMPT TO IGNITE. I read Shakespeare rather than learn to speak Italian. I never forgave the nuns their belief in redemption through, not only self-inflicted, but other-directed, pain. Or the way they made us feel the unprotected nature of our bodies. I have trouble eating dinner if a particular ex-nun is at the table. I gave, I gave, without regard for my own appetite. I had to learn how to eat again like a drooling infant: "May I have one more bonbon please?" Though I knew I resembled Bouguereau's nymph-like olive-skinned beauties who never got old, who were innocence incarnate, I anticipated a monster in the mirror in place of my face. For a time, I judged others too harshly. For a time, I was unable to enter any room but those of my own making. I couldn't trust the bricklayer if I didn't mix the mortar. I contemplated burning the confessional to the ground, but I knew it was impervious to fire. I wrote this with the conscious intention of resisting the lure of lyricism, the sentimental story. Why wax romantic about an unpretty picture? The anti-queer world. A world increasingly devoid of language capable of expressing a new thought. I secretly admired the ugliness of Gertrude Stein's prose. I wanted to make music but only so long as you didn't translate it into wash-worn forms. (At this point, Curly from the Three Stooges asks if I have a "poysecution" complex; Freud answers an "Italian American ex-Catholic lesbian is being beaten," while blowing the smoke of his cigar into Curly's face. Curly and I perform an improvisatory dance together close to the floor, requiring nonsensical props.)

A corner of the room becomes an autumn day. Turtles sun themselves on fallen branches. The river reflects nothing but turtles' slow breathing and the amber outlines of their glossy shells. Two women traverse a bridge/arc of their desire. They have pressed their ears to each other's hearts. They have crawled along the bridge buttock to belly like the turtles. They have made each other bend and relax. They have been gentlest at the small of each other's backs. The rhythm that is their love is nearly as logical as color. They have been knowing each other this way these autumns. They have been sleeping in each other's arms for centuries.

I often failed to record my visions for fear they would offend. And I wonder to what extent this is not my own but my family's legacy. Several cousins of my generation have sought the religious cloisters of Carmelite and Carthusian monasteries. They've bid good-bye to the world and taken to religion with a tenacity their ancestors could never have anticipated. Numerous others of my cousins have taken vows of silence in the form of depression: they have insuperable difficulty leaving their homes, leaving their rooms, leaving their closets, facing the light of day or the voices of other people.

I climb out of the confessional box. I am covered with confetti. I have nothing to confess. I have never had anything to confess. I send an ear-piercing whistle into the corners of the rooms where my cousins dwell. We cover each other with confetti and share our fears. We admit to having visions. We give each other a secular blessing. We are not immune to breakage or harm. We dare you to tell us you're offended. We refuse to confess. There is nothing to confess.

CHAPTER 10

Christening Scenes

To be working class was always to be in a simultaneous state of surround and transparency. Surround: my neighborhood was cacophonous with the noise of work and rage. Someone inevitably had his visor lowered to extra welding in his garage on the weekends, or a hammering job that threatened to split the fragile foundations of the neighborhood would pound out from the small fenced-in patch that was an amateur boxer's backyard. Houses did not communicate with one another so much as they interfered, in their married proximity, with one another. No community to speak of, except at church, where contributions were the key to success no one could purchase. Transparency: being astonished and embarrassed to discover that I could see my family's unselfconscious movements from the window of my friend's house across the street.

When I try to picture the street I grew up on, my mind

floods with the fear of impending violence, and all I hear is a heartbeat—but whose?—like the padding of feet down a corridor of no return. The violence of seeing and being seen. The violence of being forced to listen and being wholly heard. The violence of body opening body, of male against male or male against female. He spun him round and threw him onto the cement; he grabbed him by the shirt collar and threatened to choke him; the father beat the small boy / as the boy grew older, he ordered the father to beat him.

The baseball bat—all-American icon—was a popular battering device, and I vividly recall the day when one of the neighborhood's most frightening maniacs, baseball bat in hand, bolted through the front door of our house in search of my oldest brother who had in some way offended him. My mother, always the boldest respondent in the face of such attacks, somehow managed to lead the 200-plus-pound psycho out of the house, and away from my brother. Incidents like this were not isolated from daily life but deeply interwoven with it, and the baseball batter's was just one face among others attached in my memory to numerous violent acts directed against my brothers. One calls my brother a big-butted fairy, then slashes his school bag with a razor blade before threatening to slash his face; another kicks my brother in the balls then proceeds to steal the money from the paycheck he's just cashed. My other brother comes home one day with a hole in the center of his flesh-colored sweater—the most frightening of the neighborhood's terrorizers has thrown him to the ground and tried, for laughs, to drill a hole in his stomach with a hand-cranked drill. Both of my brothers have their new and only set of fishing rods stolen "at knife point" while trying to catch something in Darby Creek. "At knife point" was an all-too-popular phrase on the street, and when I heard it I saw a knife denting the side of a person's throat or felt a painful pinch at the back of my head. Though I had never been held "at knife point," someone did try to attack me once as I walked home alone from high school. I tried to stay at school as long as possible, immersed in the numerous activities that I craved to keep me from going back into my unhappy home. The attacker grabbed me from behind and thrust his hands into my front coat pockets. Instinctively, I threw him off using a gesture somewhat akin to one of the phony defenses I'd seen in pro wrestling on TV. For reasons I can't explain, the attacker then ran off, and when he was very far out of sight, I began to yell at him with mock confidence: "Who the fuck do you think you are, you fucking asshole?"

Such violence was not, as is stereotypically assumed in the United States, a way of life for Italian Americans per se. The neighborhood was mostly populated by Anglo, Irish, and African Americans who shared, though never exactly or equivalently, a rage-inducing class status. The people who seemed uniformly to stand outside the circles of violence, whose role seemed to be to take people away from what hurt, were the few recognizable queers on the street, the despised angels of the neighborhood.

Concord Road was a block from the hospital where most of its residents bore their children. The steady blare of sirens, the flashing yellow light, the seedy snack bar where my friends and I bought cigarettes—none of the hospital's external or internal details stood to comfort one. Too many people on the street returned to the hospital as victims of violence. Staci was a hospital worker everyone recognized, as was Mike, who lived at the bottom of the street. Staci was a transgendered African American known for his ability to make emergency room patients feel that no matter their pain, it was ok. Everything was going to be alright. "Is Staci on duty?" was the question asked routinely by people besieged by accident. Yet his walks home were never safe, and the same people he cared for allowed their children to hurl epithets at him. Mike, a white gay man who worked in critical care, saw many of the street's people through the first moments of grief after death had taken one of them away. Mike's gentleness in his care of the body of the beloved, his presence in the face of finality and loss was a well-known fact in the neighborhood, just as everyone also shared a secret knowledge they never announced about why Mike couldn't be invited into the house—because of some unmentionable things they imagined went on in *his* house even though he lived alone.

And then there was the dyke who moved Lena Di Mattia out of her house. Lena Di Mattia was one of two neighbors who had mimosa trees, uncommon company in Darby's northern clime, growing in their backyards. I loved what the mimosa trees shed: in one season, seedpods that could be rattled or opened and strewn. In another, a mat of pink flowers with gold centers, shaggy flowers that were like tassels. Tassels fallen from the headdress of a high priestess in a passing parade. The woman to whom the tassel belonged never walked unaccompanied, so important was she. In my imagination, she towered above me, easily three times my height. In reality, she was our next-door neighbor, an amateur opera singer with an exquisitely beautiful face and a limp, whose backyard featured nothing but a pink mimosa. Once I heard Lena Di Mattia sing, I could no longer picture her with a dustrag in her hand. If my mother and she spoke between house cleaning and Lena happened to be caught, rag in hand, I'd pretend it was her handkerchief, which I'd hope she'd drop so I might retrieve it. What I never failed to notice about Lena was that she always wore a touch of gold—depending on the season, a gold sandal, a gold earring, a gold ribbed sweater, and didn't her face have a golden glow? She seemed to like me; she always smiled at me and gave me chocolates wrapped in gold foil. (You couldn't get these out of a machine—they came from Italy, she said.) Once when I was forced to stay indoors on a rainy afternoon, I heard her practice her singing. Her music frightened me at first because of its volume—I felt it in my stomach and in my heart as I did my father's yelling. But the more I was surrounded by her voice, I felt something distinctly different: her voice was sweet and deep; it mellowed and melted me and made our dining room seem several times its normal size. My mother, finding me rapt and unusually silent, asked if I wanted to know what Lena sang. She brought out a book and proceeded to tell a story about an Egyptian priestess, and an Ethiopian princess, a king and a tomb. I knew that I was supposed to like opera, that my mother would like me to choose an interest in opera over rock collecting, and that opera was an important inheritance—right up there with the hedge. But I preferred our Danny Kaye recording of Grimm's Fairy Tales to opera legends, and I usually forgot the opera stories my mother told me as soon as she was finished telling the tale. In this case, though, I latched onto an image: the book my mother read the story of *Aida* from had a picture of a woman with a headdress, and the headdress had tassels that I wanted to touch.

The details that motivated Lena's sudden departure from the street were sketchy: there was a bruise on her magnificent face and talk of her husband having slept around. There was commotion, and hurry, and finally an unforgettable display of high drama on a muggy summer's day. My friends and I had been playing dodgeball—a game whose object is to avoid being hit with a large rubber ball—in the street when the car and ten-foot trailer attachment arrived. The woman driver was short-haired and burly—quite muscular really—and Lena came to the door to meet her wearing her gold lamé slippers. There was nothing sentimental about their embrace—there was important business to be done and forward motion. In the space of six hours, Lena's friend would pack, arrange, load, and tie down each and every stick of furniture from Lena's house. And for most of the six hours, I sat on our front steps, or stood tough boy–like with the dodgeball ball resting on my hip, and watched. Rapt. Sometimes I was just atwinkle with the sight of the dyke's body's force of will. The ring of sweat around her neck grew in concentric circles as the day wore on. She winked at me. Other times I was overwhelmed with what this woman's act—Lena's angel, Lena's guts—would mean for me. There was an evacuation underway. Lena was being taken now out of danger's way, but the rest of us remained stationary in spite of the threat. This lesbian angel was taking Lena off the street, and it was beautiful, and it was cruel: I would never hear Lena's singing voice again, a passion that was not a scream, a voluble kindness.

Once the story of Lena's exodus became part of the street's folklore, the emphasis was on her husband's gaping mouth and the image of his return home from work to—surprise!—the empty house, save for a coffee cup that Lena left in the middle of the dining room floor (it was an item, some said, that she was required to leave by law). I, on the other hand, remained fastened to the partnership of guts and grace that moved Lena out. "Who do they think they are?" someone might have asked, "The gall. The balls." And I wondered whether my mother mightn't have any gay women friends—who, yes, knew exactly who they were—who could help her to leave too.

In the same era that Lena's unfamiliar singing lulled me, another girl and I called to each other daily to play a special game. We'd stand in the back driveway and pretend we were kissing. First we'd act out a routine role for a man and a woman—the woman is washing a dish? the man is reading the paper?—then we'd find each other, and in a rush of distracted passion pretend to press our lips into each other's souls. Once, as we acted out our frantic embrace, we were yelled at by a gruff man with a permanent visor attached to his face. His face was hot from the interminable posture he kept over a welding flame in his garage, and the veins in his muscled arms pulsated green to match the color of his permanent work clothes. Though Mr. Welder from another planet gave us the impression we were doing something gravely wrong, this didn't stop us from finding a different spot to pursue our passion the next day, and the next. We were, after all, in love.

One day, we met beneath a sapling mimosa tree in a neighbor's backyard. This time my pretense at masculinity—I was on this day playing the man—seemed to require muscle. I lapsed into a daze, flexed my muscles and began to tear limbs off the struggling tree. This was supposed to be foreplay. I was stopped, though not immediately—because it was hard for anything to break through the circle of libido my friend and I had drawn together—by the voice of an ancient woman screaming at me from her kitchen window in Italian. I didn't know what she was saying, but she didn't pause to breathe. This woman's voice—angry, strained, and wrinkled—gave me a sick, throbbing sensation between my legs. Shocked by the thought that someone had been watching us, I dropped the branches from my hands, ran for my life, and didn't look back for my friend. An impression of her lingered, as through a looking glass, in which she had been pretending to comb long blonde tresses and to powder her face. In one instant, I snapped the tree branch; in the next, I snapped off my connection to her. I felt badly for having left my friend to fend for herself in the foggy, dreamy distance where I'd abandoned her, in reality, Anita Simonelli's rather uninteresting, unkempt, and overgrown backyard. But I felt worse about the fact that this time I had truly been doing something worth reprimanding, even if I had been unconsciously compelled to do it. I shouldn't have been destroying that tree. Alongside my father's love of gardening, I seemed to be learning something else about what it should feel like to "be the man"—to bend the bough and make it snap. The fear this episode filled me with drove me away from any further role playing with my friend.

Whenever I come upon a mat of mimosa blooms, strewn like tassels fallen from the headdress of a high priestess in a passing parade, I feel that memory as an indelible wound. Gaining a deeper knowledge of gardening doesn't help, for what the botanical guides explain is that what most people call mimosa is probably acacia. Mimosa are more rare and distinguished by their sensitivity. The mimosa will actually respond to human touch by withdrawing, collapsing so as not to be harmed.

Violence might bear a relation, the street's queer angels seemed to say, to not knowing who one was. My father married late by 1950s standards, at twenty-eight, and like so many other "husbands," he returned nostalgically in his memory to the glorious days of homosociality in the army. But his repertoire of stories about those days weren't so much about glory as they were about harm—the harm he caused other people or other creatures, the guilt over what he had destroyed rather than loved. Three short tales in particular he told over and again at the dinner table. He wouldn't make eye contact as he recounted their details—he'd just pause between bites of the drumstick he held in his hand and stare into the space above the center of the table when he told the story of the bird, and of the kidney, and of the nose drops.

In the bird story, my father, stationed somewhere in Alaska, is playing with his rifle when he accidentally shoots a bird. He goes to the bird and finds it's dead. He feels horrible to see how in an instant the bird loses its warmth because of his folly. The kidney story requires that we picture another man lying atop my father. They've gotten into something between a tussle and a serious fight, and my father explains how each time the man on top of him swings his arm upward to slug him, my father takes advantage of the opening this makes to the man's kidney, at which my father directs, repeatedly, a fierce and stinging punch. The man's kidney is permanently damaged as a result, and my father appears to feel remorse for this. My father had trained as a paramedic in the army, and the nose drop story is about a case of medical negligence. He'd placed his patient's nose drops in a cup alongside his bed and the patient accidentally drank them. My father told this story with a slight sense of humor tinged with horror and guilt. The patient suffered some discomfort, but survived.

Maybe these stories were my father's confessions and he gave them to us, as bread and wine were passed around the table, in search of absolution. But I could not forgive what I failed to understand: my father's schizoid profile. After my father kicked my brother in the ass and called him a donkey, or after he pulled at the short hairs of the crew cut he insisted my brother get, or after he whacked him one on the side of the head, or after he "belted" him one, he'd tend his roses, or prune his parsley, or check for new growth in the garden. Perhaps if my father had learned to love other men, he could have better loved himself and his sons.

My mother claimed she married my father because, unlike other men, he didn't "try anything" with her before their marriage. Perhaps she should have read this otherwise. I often wondered what she *had* desired in him. One of her dinner table stories of what-could-have-been told of Sal, a mafioso figure who came, bodyguard in tow, to the VFW dance hall where she had also met my father. Sal's bodyguard was directed to tell my mother that Sal would like the next dance. One week Sal took her for a ride and told her he could "give her the world." The next week he proposed, and my mother, mock sighing as she remembered, turned him down. When my mother told this story, I'd try to picture the world without my child self in it— who would my mother's baby have been if she hadn't married my father? And I pictured her lost life as a B-grade movie. Then my mother would explain how she wasn't immediately drawn to my father, but that her best friend, Roseann, insisted she date him because he "owned that wonderful Mercury." Both of my parents longed, I know, for their same-gender best friends, whom they saw only very occasionally and eventually not at all after their marriage.

My mother exuded sexual power and voluptuousness, and there were many occasions on which she brought me along on visits, to female as well as male friends, in the hope that the presence of a child would prevent any advances being made to her. Usually the interlude would be with unemployed poets whose floors were sticky, whose iced tea tasted of whatever else was aging in the refrigerator, who served cheap red wine to my mother while they listened to Jim Croce and read poetry aloud. My mother would always come home with flowers and books from these suitors, and more than once, to her surprise, my presence didn't stall their advances. They showed interest in us both.

My mother knew she was desirable and desiring, but she feared it. My father, he who didn't make advances while they dated, was supposed to protect her from her own passions. The same dinner table that receives my parents' narratives of guilt and longing is periodically overturned—literally overturned—by my father. I can't imagine what impels him to hold the plate of food my mother has prepared high in the air while threatening her: "I'm gonna break this dish over your head." He doesn't perform the act that his words suggest, but his trembling posture, suffused with the desire to make something or someone break, and especially the sentence he has made, horrifies me. On some level, my father never "wins" in these dinner table episodes with my mother because my mother has a better command of language. My mother's weapons are words, immensely articulate, even rousingly poetic argument. My father's is the positioning of his body in space as he stands after having jumped from his seat with his butt tucked in and his penis thrust out. If the anger is directed toward the children, he begins to unfasten his belt. If the anger is directed toward my mother, then the feeling is a reckoning with the mute reply of objects.

Everything in the house has a piece taken out of it, a chip, a chunk; everything shows signs of crude repair. The rung of the chair is breaking in the hands of a father across his young son's back. It's a perfectly placid suburban day, and the father has just finished planting spring seedlings. Wood makes a muted ring when it hits a rib, not unlike the impotent beating of a broken shop bell, a clapper kicking unsuccessfully in its womb.

Sometimes things appeared to break in the house without my father's touching them. For example, I don't remember how the rocking chair got broken in several places, but I imagine it trying to absorb the smart of belt meeting flesh; it breaks, it splinters, and Dad can never nail it back together. Parts of the rocking chair are crucified to themselves rather than glued back together. I'd swear his bowling ball is permanently swollen from its trek down the cellar stairs. While his tantrums run like a tornado through the house, he stands in one place flailing: a fish out of water, he's lost his element. He's red and swollen himself, and breathless. "Berserk," I learn by reading the dictionary, is the word for his attitude of body and mind.

In Catholic households, and perhaps more seriously in Italian American ones, two people are named as parent substitutes, potential guardian angels really, known as one's "godparents." The parents choose their child's godparents when the baby is christened, in a second birth, into the Catholic Church. Somewhere along the line in catechism class, I'd swear I had learned that one's godparents were one's spiritual guides. My parents, no doubt trying to keep their best friends close to them, chose Roseann (Mom's best friend before marriage) and Alfonso (Dad's best friend before marriage) to be my eldest brother's godparents. For my second brother, they named Roseann's husband and my mother's sister (Alfonso never married, so a balance couldn't be struck here). I was the only one who was granted a pair of godparents who were already within the family, and what's more, who were a married couple: my father's sister Bessie and brother-in-law, John. I did feel special in my godparents' eyes: it was as though, when we visited them, I got special treatment, and always received a special gift. Because Uncle Johnny was my godfather, I'm also the only one among my siblings to have a home movie version of the party that celebrated my christening.

All of my uncle's Super-8 films he had transferred to video format, and watching their successive passages can be gratifying now from a distance of so many years: here's my aunt clowning around at the ironing board in one scene, seriously sewing in another; now she's riding a bicycle, rather shakily but happily with her son perched on the handlebars; now she's picking strawberries with her sister. For special visual enigmas, my uncle appears to have used a long lens: close-ups on miniature pet turtles in their Plasticine tropical habitat; the bow on an altar boy's cassock as he fronts a pageant of other children on their confirmation day; the jack of diamonds paired with the queen of spades in an anonymous player's pinochle hand; his three boys' smiles filling the screen like a trademark logo for "The End." Some of my favorite footage in these films is the playfulness that my uncle recorded: Aunt Bessie sways and claps while her son plays a silent guitar; two brothers draped on a couch play, quietly, sleepily, a board game called "Robin Hood" balanced between them on the middle cushion; a three-year-old cousin wearing a plaid suit and bow tie performs an hilarious dance using nothing but the top part of his body. My christening party is the last film on the loop, and in spite of the comedies that precede it, it unfolds, or more properly sputters as most home movies do, as a horror film with its own particular brand of violence.

Several obligatory shots punctuate both the beautiful and unexpectedly ugly movements that this film tracks. There's the pyramid of family figures squashed into the screen as they pose with the newborn in front of the house. (And here I notice that my Sicilian grandmother looks depressed; she doesn't stay in the screen long; she's the first, and she's aproned, to turn her back to the camera and go back inside the house. And here I notice too that my Campobassan grandmother can't get enough of the camera; she's wearing one of her favorite hats and posing with her head slanted to one side; she's the last to break the pyramid of people). There's the dining room table stretching like a stretch limousine. Almost all of my uncle's films include some visual mention of the habit of eating. The camera appears to be on a tripod in these shots where people unselfconsciously pass dishes, slice intently, swallow. At one point, the camera cuts to an amazingly beautiful scene of my mother dressing me: Her glasses keep sliding down her nose; she pushes them up and pulls my arm through my sleeve. She's talking, but I don't know now or then what she's saying. Her dress is taffeta; her pearls are pearly. I look at her, she smiles at me, and then we are wondrously eclipsed by the meeting of wine glasses toasting in place of our profiles, filling the screen with light. The long lens comes into play in this film too: once to capture baby rocking, face forward, against Grandmom Rose's chest; again, in a long, long take for Super-8, of nothing but my Aunt Bessie's face: smiling, talking, wallpaper, eyebrows, collar, aquiline nose, until the film seems more and more about my uncle's desire. Another scene is disturbing for what it shows: my oldest brother trying to hug my father. My father pushing him by his bottom away. My oldest brother trying to sit next to my father on a triangle of large hassock. My father moving over, moving over, rather than taking him into his lap, instead he clasps his hands in front of him, refusing to touch him, refusing to look at him. But even this isn't as disturbing as the scene that comes later to the film's day.

Aunt Bessie is surrounded by her grown sons now, sandwiched together on our tiny couch. Uncle Johnny pulls the oldest son out of his place next to his mother, sits down next to her himself and begins to grab her face. He kisses her: poke-like kisses: once, twice, three times, four, five, six, seven times. She moves her head almost like that of the infant's whose party it is. She doesn't want this; she's pushing him away; she's helpless. Cut to next scene: she's planted on the couch between her sons again, and she is hugging the eldest. Uncle Johnny enters the screen again, but this time he grabs her face, and slaps their son. Hard. His face whips round. He rubs his cheek and looks up at his father, deferentially. There is nothing to indicate the scene is strange. It's typical. As is the entry of my Sicilian grandfather at this point with a tray of cookies.

When I ask myself why someone would film this, I realize that they may not have intended to, and I also know that the pleasure of home (as opposed to Hollywood) movies is in their raw and candid accidents. Trying to picture someone filming this, I imagine a detached, unethical observer who should have dropped the camera at this point and intervened. But how to intervene in habits of being whose repetition made them seem right and natural?

Who might have chosen such a scene? Who composed it? Who decided *this* was what they would record? The camera, very likely, was on a tripod, trained to survey whatever might happen to cross its path in that instant. Yes, someone had to turn it on, but they did not then have to watch. I picture the camera as a silent witness. I try to read my family's lips to learn what they were saying in response, to the camera, for the filmmaker, to each other, in spite of their unhappiness, because of their joy, in honor of the occasion. I can't read lips; I can't listen hard enough even to make them say something different from what they were probably saying. Because this record's voicelessness is stranger than the fact of its unnameable witness, because family gatherings were never characterized by quiet, because something essential, something whispered would always be drowned out, I almost like the fact that this film is devoid of sound. Without their voices, I can see more clearly the gestures that make the space around their bodies distinct and the bodily postures of defense and relaxation, exuberance and retreat, that I have inherited. Without the noise, they make something between them glow. And yet, without the voice, there is unfillable absence; there is death.

Possibly worse than the literal bruising of my brothers' bodies and the regular detonation of objects in the house by my father, were the effects of the way he used his voice. Perhaps because my father yelled at rather than hit me—in his universe, my gender exempted me (in some perverse way) from being hit by him—yelling, to me, seemed the most harmful of his acts. It may even be true that his yelling made me more likely to "hear" voices for their power to heal and their power to harm. Everyone knows, don't they, that the physiology of hearing is a complex and fragile process involving tiny drums, filaments, air currents, and beautiful labyrinths? That the mechanisms by which we hear and the mechanisms that govern our balance are related? That you should never put things in your ear? Then why would an adult make multiple forcible entries into his child's ear? Why would an adult mar one of the most sacred and differentiated pathways by which his child could know the world?

A voice is a vibration and a breath, a rhythm and a pulse; but it's also a signature song with infinite tonal possibilities. My father's yelling entered me like little explosions or claps of thunder that interrupted the range of my inner voice. My father's yelling, an unholy disturbance, made my body ring. His voice sought neither gently to wake or calm but to frighten those in its midst. If you think a voice cannot act like a pointer, think again. The bursts of my father's voice struck one like a score in fencing: "a hit, a palpable hit!" Yelling can cause a listener's synapses to tear, and then it's anybody's guess what happens to the spillage and what cost repair.

If one's inner voice is in large part an amalgam of how one has been spoken to, then my father's interruptions can partially explain what I used to experience as an internal Tourrett's syndrome, which is not to say the voice of my "obsessions" is a tape-recorded trace of my father's most violent voice, but that my voices are a sign of his disturbance and a sign of my, however mute, rebellion. Talking to oneself, however, may never lead a speaker out of darkness and into light.

Maybe "profanity" appeals to me because my father had such a visceral reaction against it. My father acted as though certain words had the power to kill him. "Jerk-off" ticked off a *petit mal* seizure, "fuck," a *grand*. Utter these words, and you strip him of his defenses; utter these words and he tilts, all out of order, there's no telling what he might do, for you've undone him. His own invective—in the form of the Yell—did not rely on swear words, so-called. It was all form and no content, a use of the voice but not of its lexicon. Almost a prelingual, powerless encounter with the world, yelling, no matter its content, context, or intent, hurts me at a core. I want to say "I cannot be yelled at," but of course I *can*, insofar as I cannot not be sometime in yelling's way. Yelling doesn't kill me, it turns out, but it reminds me of a smart. If someone yells at me now—a fellow driver, a hassled bureaucrat—I experience a visceral sensation in my genitals, that sickening throb. I've never found another woman who shares this experience, though I have heard men describe a feeling of testicular retraction in the face of fear. It's as though my father kicked me there when he yelled—indeed, my father did, until my mother stopped him, kick me, as a baby, in the ass.

Even today a man's yelling reverberates through the screen into my kitchen, into my ears, down through my neck and stomach, and into my gut. I can't tell whether I have chosen the neighborhood in Providence that Jean and I have recently moved to or if it has chosen me. Near Providence's "Little

Italy," the street we live on has a multiracial, multiclass population. A few of the houses, including the apartment that we rent, are gay-owned, refurbished Victorians. Many of our middle-class friends wouldn't live here—the degree of danger and dirt is too unpredictable for them, but Jean and I feel more at home here than we would on the tree-lined east side of the city. Or do we? The yelling of our Italian American next-door neighbor is so disturbing that the woman who lives on the third floor of our house, a recent graduate of Brown University, has reported him to Family Services. He's abusing his children, she says. "Don't you hear him yelling? I can't stand it," she says. "I can't live here with that going on all the time. He yelled at his son, and then threatened him with a baseball bat." I hear him yelling; I *feel* him yelling; I recognize my father in him; I notice that his children, who are extremely dear, skitter when you look in their direction, but I wouldn't have thought to call Family Services.

One day I am forced into a more direct encounter with him. I had just wanted a photo of myself in front of the rose bush—the only blooming foliage behind our new city abode. Jean suggests we pick a few of the roses and put them in a vase. I add that, yes, if we pick them, the bush will yield more blooms. Our photo shoot has been backlit by the sound of yelling from the house next door—he has addressed everyone there: children, wife, mother-in-law, and now, leading them out the door, he for the first time—boom!—is addressing us.

"Hi Girls!" he yells. Should we respond to that address? Should we look at him? "Honey. Darling. Baby," he says, looking in my direction, "D'ya want roses? I got roses. White. Orange. Come around to the side of the house and take whatever you want."

"So now I guess we have to accept his flowers," Jean says, but somehow she gets out of the task of clipping them and slips into the house. I round the corner with my Exacto knife, wondering if he'll mistake it for a weapon, wondering if I'll have to twist it into his belly. And I think: "Why am I answering his command? How can you refuse a man's flowers? Why am I following his command? How can I refuse his flowers?"

"Take as many as you want, anytime you want them," he yells from his car as he barrels out of the driveway. His wife, in the front seat next to him, smiles the awkward smile, the isn't-he-great terrified smile of the wife of the violent man. The kids look skittish in the back seat. I, positioned mutely in his driveway, hypnotically, complicitly, cut flowers.

A few weeks later, I hear a number of loud voices emanating somewhere from behind the house. When I go out to see what it is, I find the wife and mother-in-law of the next-door neighbor grilling my landlord's elderly father, a quiet man who spends his days working on the houses that he and his gay son have rebuilt together. I ask what's going on, and why they are bothering Dennis's father. Someone called Family Services they all shout in unison, and they want to know *who*. The neighbor, addressing me from a distance of fifty yards, asks if I was the one who called? The wife talks to the air; she keeps repeating to no one: "I can't believe someone would think that he could hurt our kids. *Look* at them. *Look* at them," she keeps saying, "Aren't they beautiful?"

"They *are* beautiful," I say, and refuse to answer his question of whether I was the one who called. The mother-in-law says, "He wouldn't do anything to them kids, it's unbelievable." The black man who waxes the neighbor's car asks me if there is a "Brownie" (slang for Brown University graduate) who lives in the house. I say there is no one by that name. Meanwhile the neighbor keeps up an uninterrupted spray of screams, standing alone at the center of his driveway. He is saying something about gaining his children's respect. At which point I venture, though I should know better, a reply: "My father yelled at us, and it didn't gain our respect." It was the wrong thing to say because the neighbor only heard the first part of the sentence which now became his refrain—"*Your* father yelled at you"—as though I were agreeing with him and with his black and female bodyguards that there was nothing wrong with his behavior. Then he tells me threateningly that it is only because of him that our house has not been robbed, that he's our protection. (He has a special interest in protecting me, my landlord later reports, because he's figured out I'm Italian.)

The encounter has no resolution; its point was for us to know that we had made him mad. Soon thereafter, my feelings of recognition become more strong. I become aware of transparency again: Jean and I have chosen nothing but thin lace curtains for the three tall windows that light our voluminous kitchen. We love this room because of its light, but now I am aware that from his house, our neighbor can see right into our kitchen especially at dinner time. I'm sure our love is palpable in the meals we share together: ravioli with broccoli rabe, spaghetti with fried eggplant and ricotta cheese, Sidney's hot beet borscht, Jeannie's grandmother's Yorkshire pudding. We touch, and hold, and kiss each other before, during, and after meals. He "protects" me because we're Italian; he assumes we have something in common. If he knew that I'm a lesbian, would he hunt me down? Surround: even as I write this, my heart might leap at the sound of his yelling, and it's hard to tell if his voice is outside or inside my home.

My next-door neighbor reminds me of my father in this: he is desperate for his children's, for somebody's love, but he doesn't know how to say he wants someone to love him. He acts instead toward his children as though he wants them to know he is *boss*. And he remains desperately sad that we can never properly understand, never properly address him as boss. One does not love one's boss. On those numerous occasions when my father transported himself into a state of rage, or shook us silly with his fury, or struck some young one of us with the back of his hand, he also posed an obsessive question: "Do you know who I am?" "Don't you know who I am?" Or, "Who the hell do you think I am?" I wonder who he thought *we* were when he asked us this, as we searched his face for guidance, for should a child be expected to tell a parent who he is? I reimagine my brother, terror-stricken but open, answering my father with a child's second sight: "You're the unhappy guy who sits over there when I sit here. / You're not a fairy princess with one tooth missing; you're not a snowman with a heart of smoldering coal; you're not a grandfather clock, and you never let me hide inside your coat. / If you want we can play this game where things are not what they seem to be and we both are something else. / If you like, I guess you can hit me." My own imagined reply is almost a nonanswer. I want to say, "You are a kind of body with a powerful voice; you are an 'unnamed thing.'" I want to answer with a question: "Who does any of us think we are? Who are we?"

My oldest brother has been known to say that none of the violence in our household, none of the violence on the street, ever happened. Whereas all I ever do is remember it. I heard. I saw. It cannot be denied. And yet my memory of these histories of violence is in a certain sense void of content—I've lost what the fighting was *about*. Truly, it could have no good cause. As for my father's recollection of harm past, he does not remember it, and if he did, he would fail to see that he had done anything wrong.

Once, in my first year of graduate school, as I attempted to do psychoanalysis long-distance, I made a tape rather than put in a phone call or a letter to my analyst. Thirteen years later, I happened upon the tape again, having forgotten that I ever made it. Readying the tape recorder to listen to the cassette again, I was both intrigued and afraid to hear what I might have said to my analyst in those difficult days. My mother used to joke that in her own therapeutic sessions, she spoke some of her greatest lines, told some of her greatest stories, lost to literature, disappeared into the analyst's couch. No such pearls of wisdom are to be found on my tape, no such astonishing discovery, but, rather, a rarest of rare unselfconscious tellings—a voice that is purely a listening. It's not what I'm saying but the fact that I'm talking that the tape seems to be about. The voice has a husk and hush; at some points it is gravelly, like a spirit that is water spilling over rocks; at other points it is grave, like a girl prematurely aged. And it is kind because it believes it will be heard: "I hope that you can hear my voice on the tape," I say. I like thinking about the fact that I can say these things and that "you'll hear them and they don't really have to make sense." "I seem to need to hear from people more than other people do," I say. "I really haven't helped them in the way they need to be helped," I say of family and friends. "I have a basic need to relieve people's desperateness or to relieve the pain that their desperateness causes me." More than once, I reflect on why I feel the urge to make a tape. More than once, I express the feeling that I have "left something unsaid." "A lot can be determined by what is left unsaid," and I end by hoping that my analyst will help me hear that. I end by needing someone to listen for my silences, for what wasn't said amid the screaming.

CHAPTER 11

Don't Look Now:
Lost Children/Lost Witnesses

There are repetitions that comfort and repetitions that haunt, those that we conjure and those that are thrust upon us, and sometimes the line between the genres blurs. Between eight and ten years old, I made up my own internal ritual for falling to sleep. The external ritual consisted of my mother and I saying a prayer together; then she would kiss and hug me; then I would chant a mantra: "I love you, God bless you, you're a good cook." My mother was not a very good cook, but I wanted her to know that I appreciated that she fed me. Once the lights were out and I was alone in my bed with late-night neighborhood noises—sounds of breaking or spilling or skidding—I would picture this scene: Dick Van Dyke walks through the front door of his cozy New Rochelle house, surprised to see not just his perky wife, Laura, but friends and coworkers Sally and Buddy as well. Walking toward them with arms outstretched, he trips over the ottoman in the center of the floor. Because he is a slapstick acrobat, he does not suffer injury from the fall, and his friends pick him up, laughing. I play the opening scene of the *Dick Van Dyke Show*, complete with theme song, over and over in my head until I fall to sleep.

There *were* some pleasant, even calming, sights and sounds in Darby—the gentle roll of the nearby creek, the hospital's flashing yellow light that said "go slowly here"—but they're for poets, not eight-year-olds, to fasten on, and only retrospectively. What the unconscious throws one as a raft is probably more banal and less predictable. If I try to understand the role the Dick Van Dyke tableau played for me, all that I come up with, and perhaps it is enough, is how I thought of Rob and Laura as the perfect, loving couple, and their family, with son Richie, as the domestic trio par excellence. The trip over the ottoman and instant recovery also probably made for a satisfying closure that said all is right with the world: someone has fallen but he's gotten back up, his friends around him.

In high school, when I, for the first time in my life, began to love school (I had recently transferred from Catholic to public school), I indulged another kind of home-time ritual. Every night at dinner, I would narrate the minutiae of the day for my mother—each class, each interaction, each subject learned, each funny episode, each morsel of lunch or candy consumed—I'd restack the day into perfect order, then fan my cards to show a perfect flush of pleasure. Maybe that ritual was about bringing the order of my schooling into the disorder of my home, or about taking my mother on an outdoor journey, or about sharing my day with her so that nothing could be wholly my own. For that period at the dinner table, there was no sound but the sound of my day, all else fell away, all other sentiments could be postponed.

Every now and then I would succumb to a different kind of repetition—a memory of a preschool nightmare, the trace of whose eerie affect and soundtrack recurred. When this dream, so much like a vision, occurred, I was still small enough to sleep in a crib. I couldn't have been more than three years old. Or maybe I wasn't asleep in the crib, but, having moved on to a boundless bed, dreamt of an earlier life asleep in a crib. The dream begins with the sound of violins, a discordant melody like an orchestra tuning up. The sound scares and rouses me to wake. I can see but cannot move, and what I see is the figure of a naked black man standing at the foot of my crib and smearing it with shoe polish. I call for my mother—who I imagine can barely hear me over the sound of the violins—but when she finally comes to me, the black man—is he kind or cruel?— runs off. For a year or two thereafter, I believe that he lives in the cedar closet outside my bedroom door where my father keeps his ties. I think I see his profile etched like a pattern into the wood. It's as though the image is both a sign of his living in the cedar closet and an assurance that he will not escape from there.

A barely literate three-year-old already has access to a racist lexicon for her nightmares, her fantasies, her fears. My vision of the black man strikes me now as a complex amalgam of the grandfather I loved so much—he also polished people's shoes—the father I feared, and my desire to make a mess of things by smearing shit on my white crib. No doubt while I napped my mother was playing classical violin music on the stereo (whose dials I later broke in a frenzy of twisting and shouting as a baby), and thus my nightmare's soundtrack. Taking the (racist) nightmare and its repetition outside my individual psyche and into the street reminds me of the taboo I learned when I was dissuaded as a child from addressing all men, including black men, as "Daddy." It reminds me of the fact that the violence one really had to fear in this neighborhood was more often white on white and white on black than vice versa. Children had much to fear in my neighborhood about the death of themselves, the loss of their friends, and the brutality of their fathers. The mythologized "bogeyman" was not the source of terror, but only its pathetically clever displacement.

In the present, I occasionally have childlike fantasies about my body: my body has an upright rather than slouching posture; someone else is walking inside my body instead of me; my body is a five-pointed star, expanding or the opposite, contracting to a point in space, it is ever only a point in space; my body is separable, multiple, it can be in many places at once. Limbs rise up. In Darby, you can see bodies; free-falling, charnels at the window. They sing of where they could have roamed. Too many of the street's children are buried there, and there is no medium to release them back into their bones that they may grow, and there is no ritual that will bring them back to life.

Some deaths I only heard about and so was left to picture.

One minute the playmate was there, the next he was gone. Others I witnessed, and the sight of them I forever tried to translate into something spoken, something written, something that could be read. One young blonde boy named Terrance never came home from summer camp. The details of his murder met my ten-year-old ears: repeated stab wounds, through his sleeping bag, as he slept with the other boys "under the stars." And speculation: Did the counselors who were supposed to protect them molest the boy and then, when it was clear he would not keep their secret, kill him? Or did a marauder enter the camp and pick out this one, especially beautiful, boy to mutilate? No court of law could ever answer.

One daughter of my mother's poet friend wrote poems to my mother and brought her wild flowers. She was a tomboy like me, and though I didn't appreciate her competition for my mother, I saw in her a difference that I longed to emulate. She wore flowered T-shirts but didn't bathe much—too preoccupied with the various adventures that her solitary climbs through neighboring fields took her to. She was always going places on her own and finding things. On the cusp of adolescence, she accidentally shot and killed herself with her reckless father's gun.

In my extended family, there was even more gruesome harm to children to be reckoned with, if the loss of children can even be compared. Now *I* was on the cusp of adolescence when my family got the news of my mother's cousin's child's death. The parents were vacationing in Florida with their two boys when one of the boys, walking with his family, was snatched from the hotel corridor. The stranger slashed his throat across a Bible as though he were a sacrificial lamb. The murderer had been released prematurely from a nearby mental hospital; the boy's father, cruel irony, was a psychiatrist; the boy's mother went on to do activist work in the field of mental health, and to paint. The night of the viewing, my mother got a migraine; after seeing the boy in his coffin, she threw up inside her brother-in-law's car. And I was left to picture the choker they dressed his body with to cloak his unspeakable fate. Still a child myself, I was exempted from the "viewing," but not from what I did not want to imagine in my mind's eye.

Each of these horrors happened within earshot of my desire to get out, to get away from the street that I lived on. I did not understand yet that systems of oppression are not confined to particular neighborhoods. I thought "escape" was possible. I would be busy in my self-contained workshop of reading— like a bedraggled basement scientist trying to build a flying machine out of junk metal and fishing wire to uplift me— when someone would shake me as from a sleep, and whisper, "Listen, something terrible has happened," and this something was always more unimaginable than the last something, and we must try to console the people left behind. What happened to my eight-year-old next-door neighbor was of an even different order in its impact: This time the act was as close as our dining room, our living room, and I knew the child better than I'd known the other children who were taken away. This time I saw things, and in seeing became more of a witness than if I had only heard the violence in its aftermath.

The child's father was a semiprofessional boxer. He had a beautiful mole on his left cheek, he wore muscle shirts, and seemed self-conscious about his glasses. The child's mother had wheat-colored curly hair; she had something of the "country" about her even though she was from the "city." The child's sister was curly-headed too, and they had pierced her ears at birth. The child herself resembled an Italian madonna with a light brown pixie. She was inquisitive, unlike her father, who seemed the opposite of thoughtful, but it was clear he had singled her out for something "special," an identification with him, she wasn't to be just any girl. She was going to know things girls didn't know—he took an oddly unsexist attitude toward her. I don't know if he ever took this young child to watch him spar, but there was between them a something shared, a projection, a desire. He wasn't an indifferent parent. He was a pounder, pounding with rage. Sometimes he'd spend hours sledge-hammering objects in his backyard, or he'd thump his fists into the body bag that hung from the ceiling in his basement, or he'd repeat the beat of two pop tunes that he played over and over in his house: Elton John's "Benny and the Jets" and "Oh What a Night" by the Four Seasons. He'd usually blast these tunes at the same time of day every day, when I was in the middle of my homework, but I was always in the middle of my homework. I didn't care for "Benny and the Jets." My brother had bought me the *Yellow Brick Road* album just a year or two before (my first eight-track tape), but I found all of the songs too earnest, the lyrics too abstract. "What's a penthouse?" I used to think, and then the song would be over. But when Chickie put "Oh What a Night" on, I would take a break from my homework and work on disco steps. Here were lyrics meant for raw movement, and at the long percussive section that punctuated the piece, I would either work up a particularly intense disco frenzy or pretend I was a drummer who could pound, pound, pound. And I'd feel thankful to Chickie for playing his music loud.

Chickie was a "jealous type" and made it known that he didn't like the fact that his wife enjoyed chatting with my brother as he sat on our front steps practicing his electric guitar. I didn't understand how he could find my mild-mannered brother a threat, nor did I follow the strange way he acted when he'd ask me to babysit. More important than watching the two girls exactly were the instructions he'd give me in low, knowing tones to "watch the house" as though watching the house would be tantamount to watching the kids. "Every now and then look out the front door, look out the back door. You know what I mean? Watch the house." And I'd agree, "Yes. Ok. I'll do that." "And if the phone rings," he'd add, "you can answer it, but don't tell anyone I'm not here. Take a message." I spent most of the time babysitting fending off my fears of their hyperactive dog, named "Benny" after "Benny and the Jets." The littlest girl would go to sleep early, while her older sister, the eight-year-old, shared adventures with me and kept the dog at bay. She had an imaginary friend, she told me, whose name was "the Ache of Bactine." He lived in the basement. "I want you to meet him," she told me, and we went into the basement together while she called out: "Ache o' Bactine! Ache o' Bactine." When she said he'd made his appearance, I pretended to see him too, but I couldn't make out what he was saying. He only spoke to her. Then we'd go upstairs and watch TV until she fell asleep, and I'd carry her to bed. Chickie paid the regular rate for a babysitter, but he'd also add an extra bonus that he pressed into my palm, sometimes twenty dollars more. "Thanks for watching the house," he'd say when I'd protest that this was too much.

It was a mild October day. Indian Summer. Mild enough to have the windows open. We were seated around the dinner table when the sound of a muffled explosion coming from the street made us jump. I ran, first to the door, while my father yelled to me to stop—he recognized the sound as a gunshot. But it was too late by the time he yelled after me, and I took a multitude of screaming images in through my eyes from five different directions at once. A green junk car parked across from our front door, a man slumped down, a weapon aimed through the back window, the car speeding off. Chickie running past our doorway with his child in his arms, a bright mark at the back of her head, her body limp, he is yelling: "My daughter! My daughter! They shot my daughter!" He runs with her down the street and to the hospital. His wife, not following him on foot, but wandering from one side of the street to the other as though stricken with a terrible, sudden blindness. Her hands outstretched. The mother of one of my friends—she is in the street too, now—tries to stop Ann's mother's wandering by drawing her head to her shoulder while the mother screams an unbroken, dark, and solid "O." The child's life announced within seconds, the news announced to the neighborhood as from a disembodied town crier: the child pronounced "D.O.A."

Should we go to the police station? For some people this was a very real question—they feared for their own lives and considered not reporting what they saw. I told my mother I wanted to say what I saw, and I did, but I did not see enough to be helpful as a witness in the case, though it felt as though I had seen more than I would ever want to see again for the rest of my life. What *really* happened no one ever knew. Most of us had heard that Chickie beat up a gang member in a public place. He landed the man in the hospital that stood around the corner from our street. The gang members, angry in the aftermath of their visit to the man, decided to pay Chickie a visit. They called him to his door. He came, gun in hand, to his door. But when his wise child who was playing in the street across from his house saw him come to the door, she ran to him. As she ran, her head received the bullet meant for him. "Why did she run to him?" everyone wanted to know. Did she think he was calling to her to come in the house? Or could she tell her father was in trouble and she ran to protect him?

In the aftermath of that day, the street was hazy. I remember most how damp the street felt, for days, months, and years thereafter. And I remember the medicinal smell of the soap that spurted from the street cleaning machine that periodically made its noisy way up and down the street, bristling. Because we lived next door to the family, and because the walls were thin, we tried to keep up a respectful silence in the weeks that saw October to a close, no harvest this October but for a bloodshot sky. So many silences fell that snowless winter, but the streets were wet, wet, wet.

Sometimes the tone of a phone message bespeaks a certain hell. Just one year ago, a message, in monotone, from my brother: "Hi Mary. It's Joe. When you get a chance can you give me a call over here? We have a domestic problem in the house I think you should know about. Good-bye." When I call my brother back, he tells me that he wants me to know that he's had a fight with my father, and that my father hit him. My brother is nearing forty; my father, seventy. The argument that prompted the battering had something to do with space and air: my father is eternally cold, and needs the windows shut; my brother is claustrophobic and asthmatic, and likes the windows open. My brother dared not hit my father back but took his punches as though he were a child again, with the difference that this time he could acknowledge it to someone else as a wrong about which something should be done. This may not seem like progress in three decades, but it is. My brother was not asking me to do anything; he just wanted me to know. He wanted to shame the old man before the old man's children, who are now more adult than he. He wanted the old man to have to apologize to me and to my mother. He didn't care, he said, for himself. I cried when my brother told me this—I couldn't bear the repetition of the act. I turned angry when he told me that my father hit him in front of his children. Now they must see what I had seen, but this was worse because, I'm sure, so strange a thing.

In the hour following my next-door neighbor's murder, another little girl was lost, another child lost track of. Ann's little sister. "Where *was* she? Where was *she*?" a voice cried out. And someone found her crouched and hiding by the hedge, my great-grandfather's hedge, which extended healthily now to surround the neighbor's front yard as well as ours. Nina had been protected by the hedge, but, hiding there through it all, she had seen her sister running too, she had seen her sister fall. Looking out into the street as a teenager, I had thought I had seen the worst. I can't imagine what happened to that baby's sense of sight.

Sometimes, and especially it seems when I'm driving down an endless strip of open highway, I feel overcome with a fear of not seeing something I need to see and dying as a result. I don't trust the open spaces that are supposed to set us free. Sometimes I both fear and desire a certain blindness. "Be sure to *watch* the house," my neighbor said, and I picture myself training my gaze only on its corners, its fringes, the shadows its objects cast. Not looking where I was meant to look, not seeing what I was asked to anticipate, is perhaps what has made me a writer. Writing cannot in itself stop violence, but it can at least affirm a witness.

Had Ann reached the age of her first confession, what sins would she have to tell? And what book could the priests write who witness the whisper of the "sins" of children? Why was there a compulsion in my neighborhood for adults to terrorize children? I wonder if the children who did not survive the street imagined, like Ann did, friends, company, cushions for their pain, listeners, playmates; or did they like me, think up monsters in closets at the foot of the crib.

CHAPTER 12

Shadows in the Garden

Today I have convinced the men in the shop to open the shades providing that I close them before dark. What is there better than light?

FROM THE JOURNAL OF JOHN PETRACCA

I remember how my Sicilian grandfather, Giacomo Cappello, mourned the death of his wife, Ninfa, my grandmother. He wore black for one year and numerous days thereafter; TV was strictly prohibited as though it would throw too much light into the room or distract one from the work of grieving. So when we visited now—I was a child—we played cards, made hats out of newspaper, sat in silence while my grandfather wept. My grandfather took up a new habit: each week when my father and I brought him to our house for dinner, he would take his mute, darkly clothed place in the front passenger's seat and, almost audibly, breathily, pray. He was reciting the rosary.

Last week, my mother's sister, my Aunt Josephine, died. My aunt made thousands of rosary beads in her lifetime. After her daughter died, aged two and one half, of spinal meningitis, my aunt took to crafting the beads, and religion, Catholicism, became increasingly her life's devotion. My aunt's death was followed by news of a close friend's serious, possibly fatal illness. Trying to doze this evening before the television set— *Atomic Cafe* is on—I find myself imagining a particularly vivid, efflorescent set of blue beads passing between my fingers. And suddenly I—a self-pronounced anti-Catholic—am reciting to myself with crystal clarity the calming repetition of the Hail Mary—ten such songs followed by an Our Father. How could I know those prayers, having not recited them or turned in the direction of their predictable intonations for solace in twenty years? The memory is, to say the least, strange, sometimes charming, in what it will lose and find. Now I find a bead between my fingers, now I lose the space between the beads. And is the space of who I am in the felt-ness of bead to finger, or the space between? I like to think my ancestors can help me in times of need, so now I am calling on Aunt Josephine, her spirit still close to the earth my mother said. In my imaginary dialogue with Aunt Jo, she tells me she cannot help me unless I pray. Unless I pray . . . fill in the blank with all unimaginable disaster, loss. I tell her I can't pray because I don't believe. This is the short version of a longer dissertation on the oppressiveness of organized religion, the damage wreaked upon my psyche by Catholic training, the biases reproduced in the otherwise seemingly contentless utterances of church dogma. "Besides," I remind someone—is it just myself now? myself and my dead aunt? myself *as* my aunt?—"even my aunt who is a nun says she does not pray much: her day *is a prayer*, she says."

Still I wish for the beads. Blasphemous idolater that I am, I want their talismanic lure. Or maybe, really, I want to feel what linked my aunt, my grandfather, to earth, how the string of beads linked them to each other, how this form of meditation in repetition thematized their loss.

Rosary beads, collage journals, flowers in the garden are some of the handicraft that is my familial legacy. They are marks of something sighted, something sung when voice-lessness threatened, instances of remaking in light of trau-matic unmakings of their authors' worlds. To read them from the distance of several generations entails the translation of the conviction that they can offer me something I need to know—an inherited artistry, a labor of love, an embodi-ment—or maybe just something I need to tell.

Every year on January 6, on the Feast of the Epiphany, my grandmother, Rose, and my Aunt Josephine would meet at Wanamakers, a popular department store in Philadelphia. They would rendezvous at the store's trademark, an enormous bronze eagle, and browsing or shopping, they would in this way celebrate what is considered by some Italian Americans the day of the little Christmas, specifically the day on which the three wise men visited the child Christ. January 6, 1954, would be remembered as a profound exception to the rule. On that day, my aunt called my grandmother to say that she would not be able to meet her, that when she was putting her daughter

Janice's snowsuit on, something strange and sudden occurred. Janice's head jerked backward and she was unable to stand up. She developed a high fever. My aunt called the doctor. Janice became increasingly ill. My aunt called a rescue squad. It took only eight hours for spinal meningitis to take Janice from their midst. She died on the way to the hospital. Because Janice died on a city street rather than at home or in a hospital, her body had to be taken to the morgue, where my uncle then had to reclaim her as his own.

Family members tried to make sense of the incomprehensible loss in various ways. My grandmother blamed the industrial area where my aunt lived. Whenever she visited, she said, she found the child in her playpen covered with soot. My aunt, the more directly injured by the loss, momentarily exacted a less environmental, more metaphorical, aggressive, and superstitious rationale. She said that Janice had died because my grandfather, a worrisomely unreligious man, had not gone to communion at my aunt's wedding two and a half years before. The pain of this accusation sent my otherwise reasonable grandfather back to church. My aunt's brother, on hearing the news of Janice's death, punched his fist through a wall. My great-grandmother at unexpected moments shared out loud the thought that burdened her, much to the dismay of my aunt: "Poor Janees," she would say, "it's snowing on her." My mother and her sister Frances were given the job, ordered by the Board of Health, to burn anything that Janice might have touched that day or, if the item was not burnable, to wash it in disinfectant. They found themselves destroying the gifts they themselves had given her as a baby on this, the feast of welcome—a refusal of a second, a little, Christmas. At the viewing it was stipulated that Janice's body be separated from mourners by glass. For the first time ever, my mother's boss told her she could stay away from work for as long as she liked and thus keep at a presumed distance the terror of infectious disease.

It is no doubt true that my aunt lived with a loss from which she never fully recovered, and yet I wonder what that means: Aunt Josephine lived. Aunt Josephine made. When she looked at me, her sister's daughter, she knew I knew she saw *her* daughter, but never grudgingly, lovingly. So what would it mean to say she never recovered?

Aunt Josephine recovered enough to care for other children. She adopted a boy whose biological mother had dropped him from a second-story window when he was an infant, and she gave birth to another son, referred to by doctors as the miracle baby because she conceived him after a partial hysterectomy. In an interview on trauma, Robert Jay Lifton suggests that for the survivor "insight begins with the shattering of prior forms." A new form must be created to attach to the shocking event for which one had no experiential referent and therefore no imagery to make sense of the trauma. In the space of unfillable absence, Aunt Josephine made rosary beads and other artifacts that one might not hesitate to call kitsch. Mostly she worked with yarn and rope, crocheting brightly colored afghans, needlepointing keychains in the shape of geometrics, improvising her own imitation Mondrian tissue-box covers, and my favorite pieces—the dresses made to fit nothing other than a roll of toilet paper. Any standard-sized doll could be fit into the roll, to don the miniature sequined cap my aunt also made, and voilà: an aristocratic lady, wearing a lime green or neon orange dress, could be found gracing the back of one's toilet, and only you would know what she was stuffed with, what gave her skirt its hoop. Though my description may sound parodic of the thing itself, what I really mean to imply is the mocking if not the irony implicit in these creations of my aunt. Many of my aunt's craftings had an unutilitarian utilitarian quality. The toilet paper dress had a "use," but one would be hard-pressed to say its use was necessary, immediate, or urgent, even though the presence of the doll meant there would always be an extra roll. Suspended somewhere between pure kitsch and art, the dresses transformed the roll of paper from something useful to something decorative. Like "good art," they got one thinking about the abundance of taken-for-granted useless items produced in the name of capitalist need. In a sense, they were one instance of my aunt's deciphering her loss as a joke, the joke that was played on her, and responding not by mocking others but by mocking the emptiness at the center of objects that would pretend to fill a desire.

Within the realm of aesthetic theory, critics have affiliated kitsch with escapism and political quietism, with the duping of the working class by totalitarian forces, with cheap and superficial sentiment, with an inability to feel complex emotions, and as Matei Calinescu writes in *Faces of Modernity*, with "killing time." I imagine each tug of yarn drawn through its hole, each tying of a knot to hang an ornament by, each pulling taut of a pipe cleaner like the furred edge of a cat's ear against one's fingers, as forms of *facing* time, as ways that my aunt continued to be *in* time. If kitsch attempts to "assuage a fear of emptiness," as Calinescu argues, I wonder if the emptiness usually at issue is merely an imagined emptiness, even if an originary emptiness, or if certain forms of kitsch can suggest that an emptiness that one had only encountered or been engulfed by has now been confronted.

Teasing a set of beads out from within its blue velvet pouch like a snake charmer, I try to imagine the shape the world may have taken for my aunt after the loss of her daughter. I imagine doorways narrowing and perception funneling to a point. And a great labor required in first moving from that point, into which what used to be distinguishable as tree, cloud, house, sun, self had collapsed, to another point, and much later letting the point open to recalibrate difference, watching a new world issue from the point as though from a spring—not the same tree, cloud, house, sun, self as before but a renewed sense of being in time. I don't want to call it recovery, but change for change: the loss as unexpected call, the beads as symbolized response.

There are a great number of sides to a rosary bead, a great many ways to understand how through their crafting my aunt may have devised a poetics of loss, a way of confronting emptiness. In the face of the ungraspable, a bead is grasped, pause, and grasped again. Like learning to walk again, what has to be mastered is the movement from bead to bead. A well-wrought rosary bead is sensual as a nipple hardening between thumb and forefinger, a reattachment to sense. Though the believer is told that reciting the prayers attached to the beads will sanctify her, I think more interesting than cleansing is the idea of the rosary as something held. Rather than induce the disappearance of the self, it seems to encourage a dialogue or double-voicedness, a base line with improvisatory accompaniment? The Hail Mary that one repeats for ten counts or a decade is, for example, supposed to be accompanied by meditation on a so-called Joyful, Sorrowful, or Glorious mystery decided on from the start. Lest one get lost in the mystery, the Hail Mary returns one to ground; lest one be tempted to wallow in dirt, the mystery beckons one to stand, to fly. This is, of course, my homespun theory made from my aunt's homespun rosaries and not, I hope, an interpretation the Catholic Church would agree with. I'm hoping for a conversion not to faith but from raw materials to making, from fingered to formed.

I know that my aunt did not merely "serve" the church in her rosary making and did not capitulate to the church's attitudes toward women. She addressed letters to me with "Ms." In those same letters, she let me know she accepted my lover as a member of our family: "Hope all is well with you and Jeannie. . . . Give my love to Jeannie." As she was going into coma on her deathbed, among the few last words she thought to write on paper my mother read to me over the phone: "Thank you Mary and Jeannie for the flowers." Having spent more than her share of time on so many solitary islands of illness as a child, my aunt, I believe, maintained an independent preserve of fortitude that could not be overcome by consolatory dogma.

I cannot know what, through her rosary making, my Aunt Josephine was trying to "say," nor can I surmise what she envisioned in the solitude of her daily recitations or with groups of people in prayer. I do know that in the chapel of her own funeral mass, I failed to be consoled by the ritualized prayer that perhaps anesthetized so many there. I realized then that the Catholic church service was entirely "performative" in the sense that linguist J. L. Austin elaborates that term in *How to Do Things with Words*. It did not matter *what* the priest was saying (witness the automatic trance that the mass cast over the mourners) but *that* he was saying them. His utterances performed an act (vis-à-vis loss) without having much discernible content, especially with regard to the lived life of Josephine Petracca Falter. The mass was a perfect ritual of dissociation, the highest form of superficial feeling, the most magnifying form of kitsch. The way the candles were flickering, like the stuttering of an artificial log fire, I couldn't tell whether the flames were real or electronic flares in red plastic casing. The sound did remind me of the staccatoed coughs akin to sobs that were my pained uncle's attempts not to cry. If the person traumatized or in mourning is already uncomfortably dissociated, then artificial respiration in the form of more recognizable dissociating mechanisms may only return her back to the world deluded once more.

I see in the manufacture of the rosaries something better and more, for in my aunt's decision to make, not merely say, rosaries, she in a sense chose to handle the co-constitutive matter of absence and presence on a daily basis. Making something requiring meticulous care and imagined beauty, oftentimes prepared as a gift for friend or family, resecured my aunt's interest in living, and yet to fashion rosaries is to circumscribe a circle, a hollow, a loop made of luminous orbs. I want to say again that to make and to say the rosary are different kinds of acts. What would the poet make if the book and the pen weren't ready-made? If one chose to manufacture one's materials, would one's poetry look different? Would one choose not to make poetry at all? Rather than deposit her prayers, her worries in a journal, my aunt decided on different materials—color of beads, icons, forms of linkage—for making a journal each day. Each set of rosaries that my aunt made was an instrument for someone else to play on. I'm only sorry that the intended, the prefabricated, song could not be sung to her but to the anonymous force whose love she perhaps felt she had to earn.

If I cannot know what visions attended my aunt in her cramped living room workshop, I can re-envision rosaries I have known. The rosary of pink beveled beads I wore on my school uniform always felt like a pretend fringe imitating the fringes of the cool late-sixties-early-seventies plastic vest I slunk into after school. The mother-of-pearl rosary bracelet that my godmother gave me felt like a chameleon, changing colors with my moods around my wrist, now camouflaging, now flashing varying states of mind. A powder blue pair lay nestled like an unexpected toy in the box for storing picks inside my mandolin case. Another pair hung or hovered, a dove on my bedstead, an amulet. And the sound of beads collapsing into their pouch or into my palm comforted me like the returning retreat of water over pebbles that would not yield to it. I have to admit that saying the rosary had about the same uninteresting effect as alcohol does on me today—sleep or stupor. If saying the rosary could, like other meditative practice, encourage openness, alertness, or discipline of mind, I wouldn't know, for my childhood rosaries were more like differently purposed fetishes—one for each corner of the room—and less like exercises that properly aligned my soul for the Lord.

If I were a collagist, I could imagine hanging my old rosaries in glass boxes and labeling them with a name for the separate fetishistic purpose they served. On the backdrop that supported them, I would record a script describing the unutterable realities that they tried to keep at bay. Behind the bracelet, for example, I'd record a terrorizing rhyme that members of the Sicilian side of my family would play with me: "Round ball, round ball, pull-ee little hair. One slice, two slice. Tickle under there." While directing this uncanny verse eye to eye, the teller would first circle a forefinger into your palm, then tug at a piece of your hair, then slice at wrist, at upper arm, and finally tickle under your arm. The verse seemed guaranteed to conjure something, at first to implicate one in a magical ritual, only to later suggest that each part of the rhyme was a red herring, a distraction that enabled the teller access to a vulnerable spot. Behind the rosary that doubled as a fringe, I'd write the story of the stomach shred by family violence.

In a related exhibit, I'd display rosaries in which the icons that directed the meditator to funnel her thoughts through Jesus-impaled to Mary-ascended, from martyred son to quintessentially humbled mother, were replaced with common objects that may or may not resonate for the viewer: miniature tea bags, telephones, toothbrushes, objects of desire, of bondage, of freedom, of conception and misconception, of moment and of insignificance, with the prayer to be determined by the route the psyche took through the object. Vision would be hoped for, and worlds of change.

All is context. In the working-class town where I grew up, wooden rosaries against a nun's habit signify differently than plastic beads on a school girl's uniform. Plastic in itself isn't cool, nor wood warm. Though the rosary was intended for the faithful but unlettered masses, my aunt's decision to spend some important part of her days stringing and positioning beads onto wire may not be so far from arranging, as the poet does, words on a line.

There is a shadow in the garden whose source is out of reach. The rosary says you will walk there nevertheless. At the end of a path you will come to a wide circle. Follow it. It may return you to the original path. It may not. Leave the garden gate open as you exit. A poetry that mimicked this would be easy for the part that by some formal arrangement took a reader around and out. Harder, though, to make the words cast shadows all the while.

Aunt Josephine did not survive a surgery she was expected to survive. The doctors convinced her to go through with it: they could repair the damage left from a childhood battle with rheumatic fever. Her life would be different. She wouldn't be so tired, so out of breath. Aunt Josephine came out of surgery ok, surprised she had survived, she said, because she "had seen Janice." Several days later, Aunt Josephine died.

By now it must be clear that this writing is as much about my own struggles with loss as it is about the lifelines forged between emptiness and creativity in the lives of my relatives. In the most recent past, there was the loss of an important mentor and friend. I had been learning from Marjorie, a well-known experimental filmmaker, about the poetic dimensions of Super-8 and 16 mm filmmaking. Marjorie was, on so many levels, a model to me: she lived life fully; she managed to forge community in remote places; she made art in spite of major competing demands on her time. She was magnetic and serene. I was a younger, new colleague; she had already established a career, and not one, but several lives; she opened the door of friendship to me. In the middle of a February night in 1994 on a trip with her two-year-old twin daughters to visit her parents in Florida, Marjorie died suddenly of no discernible cause. I read and record the coroner's words, reported in a Providence newspaper, with difficulty: "I have looked at the entire body, both at the autopsy, when we first did the autopsy, and at microscopic sections of different sections. I see no abnormality." She was in her early forties. My partner had talked with Marjorie, who spoke enthusiastically of her sabbatical projects and a feeling of well-being, just a few days before on the telephone. I had planned to speak with her when she returned from Florida.

Recently, sitting through an unremarkable film in an air-conditioned movie theater, a certain segment of dialogue awoke me in my tracks. A woman's sister is stricken with illness, and the doctor, by way of telling the woman her sister is going to die, says to her, "Prepare yourself." Though I had certainly experienced the deaths of people in my life whom I knew were going to die, I couldn't fathom what this would entail—

to *prepare* oneself for a loved one's death. A wave swept over me as I pictured my psyche filled with empty rooms awaiting an unwelcome guest. And suddenly I found myself weeping, as though the doctor in the film had been addressing me, for I, too, was at that time facing the possible loss of my close friend Wally. So the doctor was saying, "You will have to do battle, ready yourself; you will be taken off your feet, brace yourself to fall." But I don't want to prepare myself. I reply, "No." And then, with a philosophical cock of the head, "There is no preparing oneself for death." Better if the doctor had said, "Open yourself. Let death in."

Maybe at the center of trauma is a condition of unpreparedness, or perhaps at the center of being alive. In Catholic traditions, one is told to prepare oneself for Judgment Day and to prepare oneself for the coming of the Lord: Uncle Sam points a menacing finger—"Are *you* ready?" At the time of Marjorie's death, I had been trying to un-prepare myself in very specific ways. I had decided to confront and attempt to give up my workaholism, the endless, the redundant, the discreet preparation I still put into teaching classes that I could have successfully taught with my eyes shut. The conjunction of the fears I was trying to face by preparing less with the utter unexpectedness of the loss of Marjorie led one of my friends to tell me I was "being tested." That was one form of rationalization that didn't speak to me, having been tested into oblivion by a Catholic girlhood and feeling none the wiser for it. I had my own rationalizations, of the cruel inexplicability of Marjorie's death, for example, especially in light of the loss that her daughters must face, the loss of an utterly devoted, creative, to say nothing of "together" mother: I told myself there was another world where harder work was called for, a world worse even than our own, that needed Marjorie even more than her two-year-old twins needed her. And, Marjorie, a generous, gifted visionary, was called to that other world's need. None of this made any more sense than an event that placed itself before me at this time that soon became the basis of a symbolizing process that might make its way to poetry.

On a foggy and dark morning in early March of 1994, the rain outside sounds like a bath filling with water. I drive to school hoping for comfort but feeling unbearably heavy until I am buoyed up by the scene of silver buckets attached to maple trees. The trees, the buckets, the winter harvester who placed them there all seem to augur a season of sweetness to come. I am tempted to go home for lunch, the way I did in elementary school, and when I arrive, there is a package from my mother in the mail that includes among its enclosures a postcard of a painting by Horace Pippin, *Maple Sugar Season* (1941), picturing the very scene I had witnessed in the morning: the trees, the buckets, the footprints of the sap gatherer like leaves in snow. Like a palm, also, Pippin's footprints can be read, a portrait of the sap gatherer established by overlapping traces, deliberate steps, meandering stops and starts. It's not that I thought my mourning was taking me into a mystic circle of the synchronous, but that I read the coincidence as a gift, I was struck by the idea of parallel witness—myself, my mother, Pippin—and from that day began to record such doublings in a notebook with the thought that at the end of a very long time, one year, two years, my collection might lead to a poem.

A number of the doublings were linguistic, for example, hearing the same phrase twice in a day like "Caesar crossing the Rubicon," the place name "Bountiful, Utah," the odd adjective "Lovecraftian." Others started as dreams that met up with experiences the next day: I dream that I must perform a flamenco dance. The dress and shoes are prepared. I can't remember if I know how to dance flamenco—of course I do?—if worse comes to worst, I'll improvise. The next day, I click on the car radio and flamenco is playing. I can see the black shoes, the red dress, the upright posture, the red-brown floor. Some doublings were very literal, like finding a twin bloom on a magenta-colored daisy plant. Others were more metaphoric or associative, as in the example of cognate afterimages: when I close my eyes I see the foliage in my garden: green stems, green leaves; when I close my eyes, I see the concert pianist's green dress. Or watching the splendid velocity, slow, of my eight-year-old nephew's bowling ball as it approaches and then ever so tentatively fells the pins. His T-shirt askew on his shoulder. The ball reminiscent of a silver marbleate bluefish hanging from a mobile in the doctor's office. Some doubles were surreal, as in the way an idle hair-tie is always accompanied by a penny lying around the house, while others were very social, having emerged as the unexpected meeting point in conversation.

I also began to notice what other poets had to say about the number two. In Lyn Hejinian's *My Life*, "Reason looks for two, then arranges it from there." Brenda Hillman, in her deeply stirring, wise, and beautiful book *Death Tractates*, had written after the sudden loss of a female friend and mentor: "and I wanted to hear just one voice / but I heard two, / wanted to be just one thing, but I was several." Robert Hass, quoting Leonard Bernstein in *Twentieth Century Pleasures: Prose on Poetry*, had said: "Two is the rhythm of the body; three is the rhythm of the mind," and in his own words, "Two is an exchange; three is a circle of energy." The clinician Robert Jay Lifton, in an interview on trauma with Cathy Caruth, had spoken of psychological "doubling in the service of survival."

What I thought I was searching for in my gatherings of two was a meeting place and a hunger—the breaking of a fast. An ambidextrous art. And yet I hoped to resist the idea of two equalling a kind of natural balance or easy, longed-for harmony: vision being equivalent to the practice of making two eyes work as though they were one; the importance of acknowledging that one leg was longer than the other. Partly, I was trying to love chance meetings or the stark contrasts that happen within an hour of one's life. It wasn't a likeness I was in search of. But the shadow cast by letters, language's light. I realized my emphasis on two was overdetermined: a grief for a pair of girl twins; a longing for the double movement of the rosary; a distinction between reassuring repetitions and the repetitions beyond our control: that the day on which the news was heard will return to meet itself into eternity. Wanting to learn to treat each day as something other than an anniversary.

My poem is not ready yet. It seems to need multiple voices and a form of orchestration. It seems to want to be a collage, but there's a question of whether I need to know more about traditions of collage or if I can use my family's forms of juxta-position to make it so. For now, I have this writing and the way in conversation it has led others to share with me their rosary beads, or prayer beads, or worry beads, and with every set a story of secret pleasure or secret pain. And I keep pulling more rosaries out of memory's sleeve. Perched at the end of the din-ner table that my father regularly overturned once sat a plastic rosary container with the kitschy rhyme: "The family that prays together stays together." For a spell in our hot, short kitchen, my mother had us try to say the rosary together after meals. It was a desperate time, and as I recall the rosary gig didn't last too long, for it failed to calm my father, and it para-lyzed us.

A separate, recent event helps me to see it from a different angle. I'm on a crowded lake beach outside of the city of Provi-dence in northern Rhode Island. It doesn't have the charms of seclusion held by the southern beaches, and here there's no surf to drown the noise of one's neighbors. I'm finding the number of people, the volume of squeals overwhelming, claustropho-bic. It's clear I won't be able to read here or to rest. Suddenly, whistles are blaring and muscled men and women are pound-ing furiously, running in one direction on the tiny beach. They've ordered everyone out of the water and have an-nounced a missing child, nine-year-old Jamie, her ponytail, her flowered swimsuit. Hand to hand, they've linked them-selves to form a human chain as they walk the length of the lake suspecting that the missing girl has drowned. Behind my sun-glasses I am crying. I can't seem to stop my tears. Midway down the length of the roped-in swimming area, the searchers are halted by a voice from the loudspeaker announcing a "positive I.D." Jamie has been found frolicking by a hidden corner of the concession stand. My tears, I sadly realize, are partly tears of surprise and relief that other people will look for you if you are lost. They will make of themselves a rosary. Rather than say the rosary, my family should have gone for walks hand in hand. We should have walked and walked.

Flower Rituals
across Fences and Generations:
The Night-Blooming Cereus

*Dr. Kate Bornstein, a medical doctor and molecular biologist,
was introduced to* Selenicereus *by her mother, who would rouse
her children from their beds on Long Island just as the family
plant, given to her by Edward Steichen's daughter, was about
to bloom. "The neighbors would come over and shine their
headlights on it," she said. "You can physically watch it open
within the space of an hour."*

FROM AN ARTICLE APPEARING IN THE
NEW YORK TIMES, DECEMBER 27, 1992

*June 23, 1943. It is hot and clear. We are all set out in the yard
looking at my cereus plant that its bud is showing signs to open.*

We have been waiting for the blooming for many weeks. Thank God, now we can admire this remarkable flower. It is now about 12" long and very pretty. It is eight o'clock and is beginning really to open. Here are a lot of our neighbors lovers of flowers to see this remarkable flower. Nine thirty and it is fully opened. It is a gorgeous flower. We are all pleased and astounded. Nature really can work and bring out fancy marvels. It is dark now but we still, regardless of the black-out, are nearby it. The black-out is over and the flash lights are showering it.

FROM THE JOURNAL OF JOHN PETRACCA

I was lured by that eccentric phrase—"family plant"—to understand its meaning. Like Dr. Kate Bornstein, I am moved to use this phrase to describe the Night-Blooming Cereus that have been tended and ritualized, clipped, potted, planted, and passed on among members of my family, myself included. Perhaps each gardener has his prize—the plant that he needs most before him in certain seasons, or the plant whose flower is one part labor, one part the secret letter he has sealed into its leaves like a kiss. Even gardeners whose work ranges across species, who can equally nurture flora that ask for full sun or deep shade, seem to have an obsessive streak: the single flower they fetishize or reserve for special worship. Plant lovers who devote themselves to one kind of plant—I've known some who grow *only* azaleas, dahlias, orchids—are just more willing to admit a desire that most gardeners share for singularity, the garden a proliferation of a truth, a home away from home. I think the "family plant" must be different from the plant that carries the onus of the gardener's private dreams and fears, though it, too, is among the overvalued blooms among his crop. Probably there are instances where the gardener's prize doubles as the family plant, in which case the flower's symbolism would be even harder to read.

The family plant does not share with the family a proud or loathsome genealogy, and so I don't imagine it functioning like a coat of arms to signal lineage, property relations, or an obsession with kinship. The family plant is the plant that a collective of people, bound together against their will to have meaningful relations in preconditioned ways, agrees to incorporate into their meetings as a sign of excess—the desires that will always exceed familial relations: in my family, the love we wish we could create in place of violence. When holidays fail to serve the inchoate needs of the family as failed community, there is always the family plant—more likely to blossom if given the proper care. The family plant is a form, and that's what draws the family with its formal reservations and formless needs to it. At its best, the family plant is an experiment in form, for no matter how we try to shape it, the plant is also organic, a living thing, a living thing with a life and death of its own, and so you never know what shape, or when, or if, its flowering will announce. I like to think of the Night-Blooming Cereus as a sign of my family's agreement to live. The family plant is a cup into which familial silences are stirred, the sight of which we gather around to see transformed but not transcended, the sudden burst of their expression, and the death of a moment in which we have agreed to live together. The flower fell into our neighborhood like a shooting star.

As far as I know, the Night-Blooming Cereus first appears in my family in my grandfather's garden. Coming upon a journal entry where he describes the plant's ascent is almost better than finding the flower itself, for I love the way his language blooms. Through his writing, I can dwell in his garden again; each word and the pauses between them wend an atmosphere for me to breathe in as though I sit beside him twenty years before my time, patiently awaiting the changing form he has in some part willed. Certain words flicker more or less brightly through the screen of the past: "We are all set out. Showing signs. Waiting. Lovers of flowers. Pleased and astounded. Work. Fancy marvels. Dark. Regardless. Black-out. Flash lights. Showering." It is easy to read the last two lines of the entry—"It is dark now but we still, regardless of the black-out, are nearby it. The black-out is over and the flash lights are showering it"—as a paean to a generalized steadfastness. But I also realize that the language of blackouts has special resonance in the context of the war, air raids, fallout shelters, "bombs falling on my beautiful Naples," a special meaning in the context of the periodic loss due to poverty of the electric lights by which my grandfather plied his trade, and that flashlights could be turned on any immigrant to the U.S.—Japanese, Italian—(it was a question) during the period of the Second World War. Maybe the Night-Blooming Cereus and the ritual it engendered helped my grandfather to reimagine blackouts, flashlights, and their wielders as benign.

I have my grandfather's journals, but my family did not inherit his Night-Blooming Cereus plant. My grandmother found the plant ugly, so maybe that is why it wasn't "passed down." Or maybe because my immigrant ancestors didn't quite know how to share their wealth—that would require that they first recognize it—my grandfather's plant did not take up residence in my father's garden. That the plant persisted as an idea—and thus as "family plant"—made it likely to find its way into our garden nevertheless. My immediate family gained its Night-Blooming Cereus, the plant I witnessed growing up, over the fence that marked the border between classes on our street because my mother recognized the plant, and in her expressed love for it, received it once again.

Ed and Mabel Engels lived one block over from Concord Road on a street appropriately named "Golf Road," for it was astonishing how, in the space of a block, socioeconomic class shifted upward. The grounds of Ed and Mabel's imposing house spanned the length of ten of Concord Road's backyards, to which they ran parallel. Our backyard met the Engels's grounds just closest to where their driveway and the back of their house began; my father's garden was a sea of wonders in a wasteland; my mother drew interesting people magnetically to her. These are some of the reasons I imagined for why we were the only people on Concord Road who had ever glimpsed, and beyond that, spoken to the aging couple who lived in the largest house on Golf Road, the people who gave my mother the cereus plant that I later inherited.

At the risk of stereotyping middle-class Anglos as reserved and Italian peasant stock as loud, I must tell what I remember about Ed and Mabel Engels: they were quiet people. Ed and Mabel were quiet, gentle, nice people. I saw when my mother spoke to them—she'd be holding cut flowers in one hand and a small pair of scissors in the other—that something softened in both directions. My mother was fond of these people and they of her, and when they talked over the fence, I could see that each lifted the other out of a dullness. It was all about suspension. Ed wore beat up sneakers, whitish gray, drooping pants held by a thin black belt, and a white T-shirt when he worked in his yard. I hadn't really ever seen anything like this man. He was dressed like a boy but his hair was gray, and he had a boy's gray haircut. Mabel wore subtly colored flowered shifts when she walked in the yard, a straw hat to keep the sun off, and reading glasses that hung like a smart necklace around her neck. My mother wore one of her repertoire of bookish T-shirts—with portraits of either E. Dickinson, E. A. Poe, V. Woolf, G. Sand, Beethoven, or, her favorite, Neanderthal Man, printed on the front, across her large breasts—with a knee-length, maroon polyester skirt. (For a few years in the early seventies, my mother wore this outfit in all seasons.) I don't know why I must describe what the three of them wore when they met except that together they made a garden party, and one should always know what at a garden party people wear.

Mabel fell into the category of a small handful—all of three—intellectual women whom my mother found in the neighborhood who became her friends. One was an African American political activist who worked on interdenominational antipoverty, antiracist, and feminist campaigns; another was a progressive white woman who schooled her children at home; and the third was Mabel, who was an artist. Despite their very different personalities and locale, all of these women shared a quality I strove to emulate (though perhaps never learned how). Serenity. Not "peace," but composure. A piercing certitude that gave their bearing an aura of calm. I guess they were beatified in my mind, my local saints.

During one conversation about books and flowers that Mabel and my mother carried over the fence, my father could be heard in one of his fits of rage, howling in the background. I stood by my mother; we stood where we stood. But Mabel jumped backward, and with her hand on her chest exclaimed, "Oh, my word! There he goes again. I hear that man yelling all the time. Why just yesterday while I was eating lunch I could hear him as though he were in the same room with me, and I jumped out of my chair." Dignified, horrified, disgruntled, she put the question to my mother: "Who *is* that man?"

"That's my husband, Mabel," my mother replied.

And Mabel, crestfallen, still shocked, looked back at my mother: "I'm *so* sorry," she said.

"*You're* sorry." My mother made a joke of it.

Mabel looked thoughtful then, confused; she looked away from my mother and mused aloud: "But he seems so placid." I wanted to say, "That's because you only see him in the garden," but I did not share my wise observations with adults, just as I knew on an unspoken level that Mabel would never see my father yelling because she would never come inside our house. She was my mother's friend—they touched something in each other—but the friendship did not override the trajectory of propriety that pointed us to face in the direction of Mabel's house but that could never have her backsliding into ours.

I remember once or twice visiting Mabel's house because

she invited my mother to see her paintings—realistic oils, tinged with impasto, of flowers and faces. Mabel used to look at me across the fence as though she saw something; and more than once she asked my mother if she could paint my picture. My mother thought this was a fine idea, but Mabel sought my permission too, and I was never bold enough to give it. Mabel would ask if I would "sit" for her; I would fall silent, and shyly turn away. "Ah," she would say, "I would like so to paint your portrait." Later I would ask my mother how long she thought I would have to sit and if I would have to be perfectly still. My mother thought I could probably move and that it would be a nice experience, sitting for Mabel, but I was afraid I could not sit still for so long. Would I be alone with her? Would we talk? Would my father scare us both out of our skins and ruin the portrait? Mabel could not compose me if I could not compose myself. And I didn't dare try. But I wanted to. I wanted to see what kind of picture Mabel would make of me if I sat for her. Never doing so might have been akin to my refusal of ballet lessons, it was an entry into a world off-limits. But where I never desired ballet lessons, I did long for the chance to spend afternoons alone with our neighbor the artist. Each year when she asked, I'd say "maybe I will," but she was already aged when she asked, and with not much time left to wait for me, she died. If only Mabel could see me now. How long I sit at my writing desk composing myself, composing my family, and now, in some small corner of a canvas, composing her. She would see my apartment, its disarray; she would recognize the Night-Blooming Cereus plants that overrun its edges and climb its walls, offshoots of her husband's greenery.

Ed's Night-Blooming Cereus plants, eight healthy scragglers spiraling upward from narrow pots, grew alongside one another, flush with our backyard fence. When they bloomed —and they bloomed profusely—their flowers always fell over the fence and faced our yard. My mother studied the buds until she was able to predict the night on which they would shine for us and then, by the next morning, die. Dinner would be prepared with excitement on those evenings, dishes would go undone, and I would be allowed to stay up with my mother and wait for the flower. Cricket sounds were more piercing in the yard in the pith of the night, and I always expected in approaching the Night-Blooming Cereus that we might disturb the rare flying creatures that would come to pollinate the flower, creatures I both longed and feared to sight. Ed would come out of his house at some point, strain to bend over the fence to see his flowers, aim a long-handled flashlight at a bloom, smile, and retire. But my mother would stay in the backyard for hours. Studying. Wondering. Writing. Celebrating. Witnessing. When it became clear that my mother was more interested in the plant than the owner was—who also didn't seem to want to be interrupted from sleep every time one opened—Ed gave my mother a plant that my father could tend for part of the year in the backyard before taking it inside for the winter.

Once we had our own plant, my mother's rituals became more elaborate. She would line up her collection of homemade drip candles welded to wine bottles of varying shades and shapes in erratic zags before the plant. Muted light seemed to suit the plant better, and since the flower had a lunar lambency about it, it seemed ridiculous to try to illuminate it artificially. There was no point in competing with it or forcing it to shine. The idea was to watch and wait. Soon a small handful of interested neighbors would join us in the yard (I could never tell if they were genuinely interested in the flower or if they were curious to see if they had a satanist for a neighbor); poetry might be read; and if other children came, we would reach together into a bowl of pretzels we could hardly see and suck their salt while watching. At a certain point, my mother would take me in to bed or, if I was older, tell me to go to bed now. She would come into the house with me and put the coffee on for herself, then return to sit with the flower, for how long only she would know.

Reading about the flower, I would learn that it is native to the West Indies, where thousands of flowers attached to plants forty feet tall might bloom in one night, and that moths pollinate the flowers. The odor from the one or two flowers our plant would yield every year was so overpowering that it fell like a cloying mist over the entire backyard, drenching and drugging us. The scent of a thousand must cause a seismic shift. What my mother taught me about the plant was a somewhat different knowledge. She called it a thornless cactus (which it was, more like a succulent, but to call it a thornless cactus was provocative), an earthen star, a heartbeat. She claimed that bats pollinated it, not moths. She spoke of it summoning us, or summoning someone, possibly us, so that I came to think of the plant both as something we need witness and something that might witness us. I didn't know then how the plant functioned for us outside of its being a grand event tinged with magic. Now I consider it as a symbol in the dreamspace that was my family's garden into which we collectively poured our fears and desires, for one never cultivates a flower without also provoking a dream. The Night-Blooming Cereus was one expression of my mother's passion; it summoned her into open spaces; it tempted us not to fear being alive even as it lived and died before our eyes. The Night-Blooming Cereus was my father's yelling temporarily transmuted into a loud flower. On the night it bloomed, the street's children could safely play or doze "under the stars," under its stars. That's how our ritual functioned. The Night-Blooming Cereus was pollinated by poets.

With the same conviction that most Italian mamas said to their children "*Mangia! Mangia!*" (Eat! Eat!), my mother told me in English to "*look.*" She was always commanding me thus, with exuberance, and especially before flowers and paintings. Winter has its colorful berries too, she would show me. Appreciate. Love. Live. Remember. Remember what you see and it will be a life in you, a flame turned to low, and it could be a bounty you could give to others. One must always retain the capacity to be astonished.

In walks in the woods with my girlfriend, I find myself doing this spontaneously. "Look!" I say, about practically every feather and fern, leaf and light. Quite frankly, it gets on my girlfriend's nerves. When we go for walks, she tells me, she doesn't want to be told to look at things. She doesn't trust my childish excitement—she knows I'm an adult. She can't stand the way I act as though I've never before seen a bird when one appears. It's not as though she doesn't see things or isn't interested in looking. She prefers that we walk together in silence, and then, in the space of the degrees of risk and comfort we create between us, something emerges, something is sighted, she quietly finds something to show me that I've never before seen. There's a funny way in which the mode of looking I learned by watching my family, if observed from this angle, was too noisy to enable the concentration required to see things. My mother's imperative "Look!" did take ascendancy over whatever one *had* been looking at, and I can also understand my writing as an assertion of what I might have tried to see or wanted to see amid those interruptions. This is not to say there was a conspiracy of looking in my family, but that it's hard if not impossible within a family to let multiple forms of seeing, variant ways of seeking, coexist. One form gets favored like a favorite flower, and sticks. Sometimes that imperative to look, I think, might have been a way of holding. Of holding reality before you because you know that otherwise something, thick and bright and painful as the sight of blood, will spill onto the canvas, something will be torn or broken. It's a kind of earnest looking whose base is desperation. Watching the Night-Blooming Cereus for a spell perhaps released my mother from the necessity to look.

But the Night-Blooming Cereus never held the place of an unflinching totem in my family. The way the flower functioned for my mother was different from the place it took up in my grandfather's world, just as my relationship to the flower has different significance than it did for them. The Night-Blooming Cereus has become something of a magic wand with no right way to use it. If something familial endures in its having passed between generations and across fences, it is wonder.

I carried my Night-Blooming Cereus plants over the thresholds of the hallowed halls of academia, into the spaces of "learning," the rooms designated for leisurely thought, into the groves of contemplation where no one from the street I grew up on was ever encouraged or expected to dwell. That the plants never bloomed in four years of undergraduate training, one year of teaching high school in Princeton, New Jersey, five years of graduate training through to a Ph.D. in English, and three years at a prestigious university as an assistant professor, did not trouble me. My grandfather had tended one of his cacti for thirty-four years before it gave him its first flower. Rome wasn't built in a day; social change occurred at a painstakingly slow rate over millennia; and psychological change felt as though it happened at even more sluggish intervals. Why should flowers be any different? I reminded myself of the lesson of my family's gardeners: the gardens I grew up in stood for willfulness, patience, and an abiding love of changing forms. My Night-Blooming Cereus showed its first bud in the dining room window of the mill house I was renting in Wakefield, Rhode Island, where I had begun my second academic job in order to be closer to my lover, who at that time was teaching in New York City. Prior to this move, we'd been commuting weekly between New York City and Rochester, New York, to see one another. Now the distance between us was beginning to close.

Night-Blooming Cereus buds take several weeks to develop fully, and sighting one on a plant does not guarantee a flower. The early stages can be tentative, and according to my mother, if the bud looks too pink rather than mildly milky white early on, it will probably not survive the early stage. The bud begins as the tiniest spear-shaped head that emerges literally from the side of a plant's leaf. I have noticed that the leaves, which are already thickly veined entities, almost like human arms pumping with blood, seem to get veinier in the place where a bud appears. It's as though all of the plant's energy rushes to this spot as in orgasm or birth. Within two weeks, a tube—which always looks to me like nothing other than an umbilicus—follows the bud out from the leaf. As the tube gets longer and longer, the bud gets plumper until it appears a huge, tear-shaped piece of fruit protected by the pinkish tendrils that now encase it as well as the faux "thorns" that gather at its base. Several days before the flower opens, the tube can bend upward at a ninety-degree angle, making me want to understand the architectonics of plants, their gravity, their relation to space, their ability to hold themselves up. Does the plant have an internal oxygen pump or does it just "naturally" crane toward the moon?

On the night that my plant first bloomed, a friend and fellow academic from New York who enjoyed throwing tarot cards was visiting us. I had called my mother nightly with descriptions of the bud to see if it sounded as though this would be the night. If a circle the size of a pinhole appeared at the point where the petals met, then the bud would bloom that night, she explained. It was very dark, the moon was out, and it was coming up to nine P.M., but still no sign of opening. My friend suggested she read my cards—the flower would surely bloom the next night—but we still sat in semidarkness with only candles lit, hoping not to confuse the plant. I didn't know until my friend explained it that tarot readings were not about fortune-telling so much as they were about providing a person with a hermeneutic for approaching a particular question in her life. The cards that turned up did not simplistically "predict" a future so much as they provided a sign whose interpretation, with the help of the reader, could possibly shed light on a problem. I don't remember what question I posed, though externally I was, predictably, preoccupied with the matter of whether I would get tenure at the university I had recently transferred to. The cards kept coming up with golden faces, and Barbara, my reader, beamed and laughed and said with a degree of pleasure in the text: "You have everything you need." Poised on the crest of goldenness, I recognized a heady, thick, musky aroma: the flower had been opening alongside us as if to confirm the sign: "You have everything you need." I felt as though it were my birthday, and I wanted to blow out the candles and hug the flower against my breast—which of course I didn't do. I never, until recently, felt as though I could touch the flower and was always appalled when people who didn't know better would do things like rub a petal between their fingers to see what the flower felt like. Its process mustn't be intruded upon, its pulse must not be impeded, but only admired from afar. If you mistreated your cereus flowers, they might not come back. That night, as ever after, the flower gave way to a party; a new friend who hadn't felt inspired in a very long time wrote a poem; Barbara threw more cards; another friend had an asthma attack and had to leave; others said

"Thanks but no thanks" to the invite to crawl out of bed to watch a flower. If I had told them that the flower's white petals were each one a feather, that its center was a mesmerizing spool of yellow harp-strings laced with pollen, and that out from within that depth emerged a separate figure in the shape of a star, would they have come? I guess you're either a flower person or you're not.

On numerous occasions thereafter as I struggled with my own uninteresting but no less debilitating brands of anxiety and depression, Barbara's words would echo in my ears: "You have everything you need." And if I have everything that I need, I would ask myself, why do I turn back in the direction of well-worn neuroses and numbing fears when faced with a new challenge in my life? How do I tap the everything? Want and need were different—maybe there was the crux of the matter. Having what you need and making something of it were worlds apart. Having what I needed distinguished my life from my immigrant ancestors'. How does anyone know she has what she needs if the world is still wanting?

In Dr. Kate Bornstein's story, her neighbors come to the Night-Blooming Cereus with their cars' headlights shining, as if into a drive-in movie. The rituals that Jean and I carry out around the Night-Blooming Cereus are a kind of experiment in light: every year we backlight the flower differently and photograph it. Every year its drama unfolds on a differently lit stage. Every year it offers an excuse, when we least expect it, to throw a party. Every year it offers an occasion to tell someone who has not heard it yet some part of the family story that takes me to the Night-Blooming Cereus. Every year our relation to the flower becomes a little more eccentric: I don't tell anyone that the secret to its flowering now is the way I rub its leaves after a session of Tai Chi, though people have glimpsed the botanical charts that Jean has started to make, complete with measurements and illustrative sketches, in an attempt to predict more accurately the night on which it will bloom. Every year someone is uncouth enough to suggest that this is what lesbians do in place of having children.

What's true about the flower is that it's queer. In Freudian terms, it's polymorphously perverse. Undomesticated, it fails to grow in a containable direction, and one wrong pruning can prevent it from yielding a flower. Our living room has shrunk and shrunk so it might move in all directions. Anyone who sits on the couch looks as though they have tentacles growing out of their head—spiny tentacles punctuated by scrawny tufts root like undesirable chin hairs. (The Pottery Barn won't be marketing such plants anytime soon.) It's a witchy, bewitching, hideous monstrosity of a plant. Whose flower is magnificent.

Almost always after a Night-Blooming Cereus party, some flower lover in the crowd asks me for a cutting, and almost always my conversations with them in ensuing days, months, and years is the same. They tell me about how the plant—which is hideous—is threatening their relationship, whether straight or gay, because there is nowhere in the house where the plant is welcome. They ask me what to do when people visit—can they have pictures of my flower so that they might show people that there is a reason for keeping this thing? Mainly, they want to know, how long do you have to wait for the goddamned thing to bloom?

The Night-Blooming Cereus must be a family plant because nobody else needs to put up with it in quite the way that I do. To love this plant, you might have to have memories of your mother rousing you from sleep to something even better than your dreams. You must have to have grown up in a hopeless neighborhood where nothing was meant to bloom.

Every year, Jean and I say that this year we will stay up long enough to watch the flower's final drama. We have watched it open, but what stages must it pass rapidly through, and beautifully, even as it dies? Every year, we miss its calling, the secret of its life; we let it drug us and then we sleep through its nodding bow, its star turned downward. Maybe someday, my mother, who I am sure has seen the beloved flower die, will tell me what that looks like; or, better, someday, I will have the strength to watch.

ACKNOWLEDGMENTS

No book is a solitary enterprise, and the coauthors to whom I am indebted are innumerable.

The coalition of painters, filmmakers, and writers who made up the Providence Group in 1996–97 provided the best kind of supportive challenges and inspiration for this work. In particular, I would like to thank Jennifer Manlowe, Karen Carr, Russell Potter, Nancy Cook, Paula Bolduc, Jim Hersh, Arthur Riss, Nina Markov, Miriam and Eric Riss, Sheri Wills, Marie-Christine Acquarone, and Monica Allen for being with me during some of the most difficult junctures of this book's creation.

Peter Covino, lovingly and with a poet's ear, translated extensive portions of my grandfather's journals; and Edi Giunta—confidante and brilliant critic—did the same between preparing Pastina for her daughter, Emily, and putting Emily to bed. Additional help with passages in Italian were provided by URI undergraduate, Sara Cicchelli, and by my friend, comrade, and teacher, Wally Sillanpoa whose (domestic) interiors, politics, humor, and love inspire what I create and what I hope to create.

Marianne Killilea granted me access to her extensive garden of dahlias; Rosie Pegueros granted me access to her extensive gardening library; Terry DeShefy-Longhi shared her master's thesis on Italian American immigrant gardens. Stephen Barber teaches me daily how to cultivate orchids and friendship.

Sharon O'Dair gave my writing on class more than one forum. Sally Drucker, Anthony Tamburri, and Jerry McGuire anticipated this book by soliciting pieces of nonfiction from me on gardening, sexuality, and loss. Sharon O'Brien, William Andrews, and Alane Mason coaxed me to draw from those essays the foundation for a book.

James Morrison, from whom I learned to write by listening to him speak, patiently read and responded to portions of this book in its loose and baggy, early, tentative stages.

Deans Winnie Brownell, Stef Rogers, and Provost Beverly Swan of the University of Rhode Island provided the institutional support that made this book possible, and my undergraduate and graduate students provided the dialogue that spurred this writing on.

Deb Chasman is a writer's dream: an editor who is also an artist, an editor with a vision. I would like to thank her for the mutual trust that she enabled to unfold between us, and for helping me to see the shape of the whole. I am grateful, too, for the energy and insight of my agent, Malaga Baldi.

Louise DeSalvo's generosity in encouraging this book

through to publication is unsurpassed. Her conversation, letters, and "voice" have guided this writing and filled me with pleasure.

I also want to thank Sidney Shupak, surrogate father, and friend who reminds me daily that where there is art, there is life; Jean Walton, with whom I share a life's work, for not letting me write a disembodied book, and for calming my fitful slumber by finding our book's title; the people whom my grandfather names in his journals, Mrs. Hudson, Miss Demetriades, Mr. Cross, and all other kind strangers who helped him to survive in a new culture, and who refused to discriminate; my immediate and extended family, who, I hope, will forgive me for remembering: may they give me their versions of our shared past someday soon.

The rhythms of my mother's poems, which I, from an early age, memorized, are the heartbeat of the sentences herein. *La lotta continua.*